THE WILD GOOSE CHRONICLES

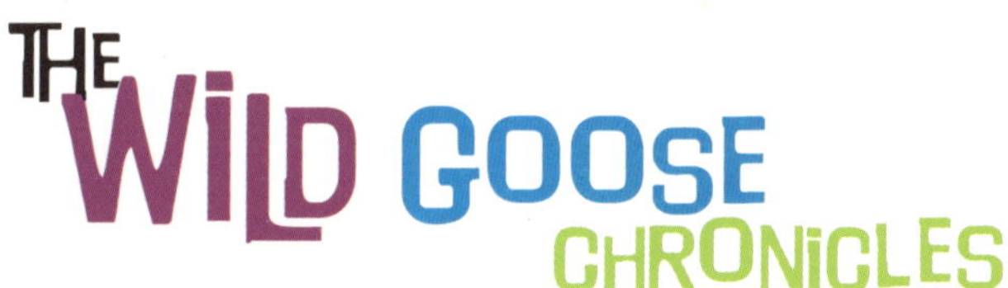

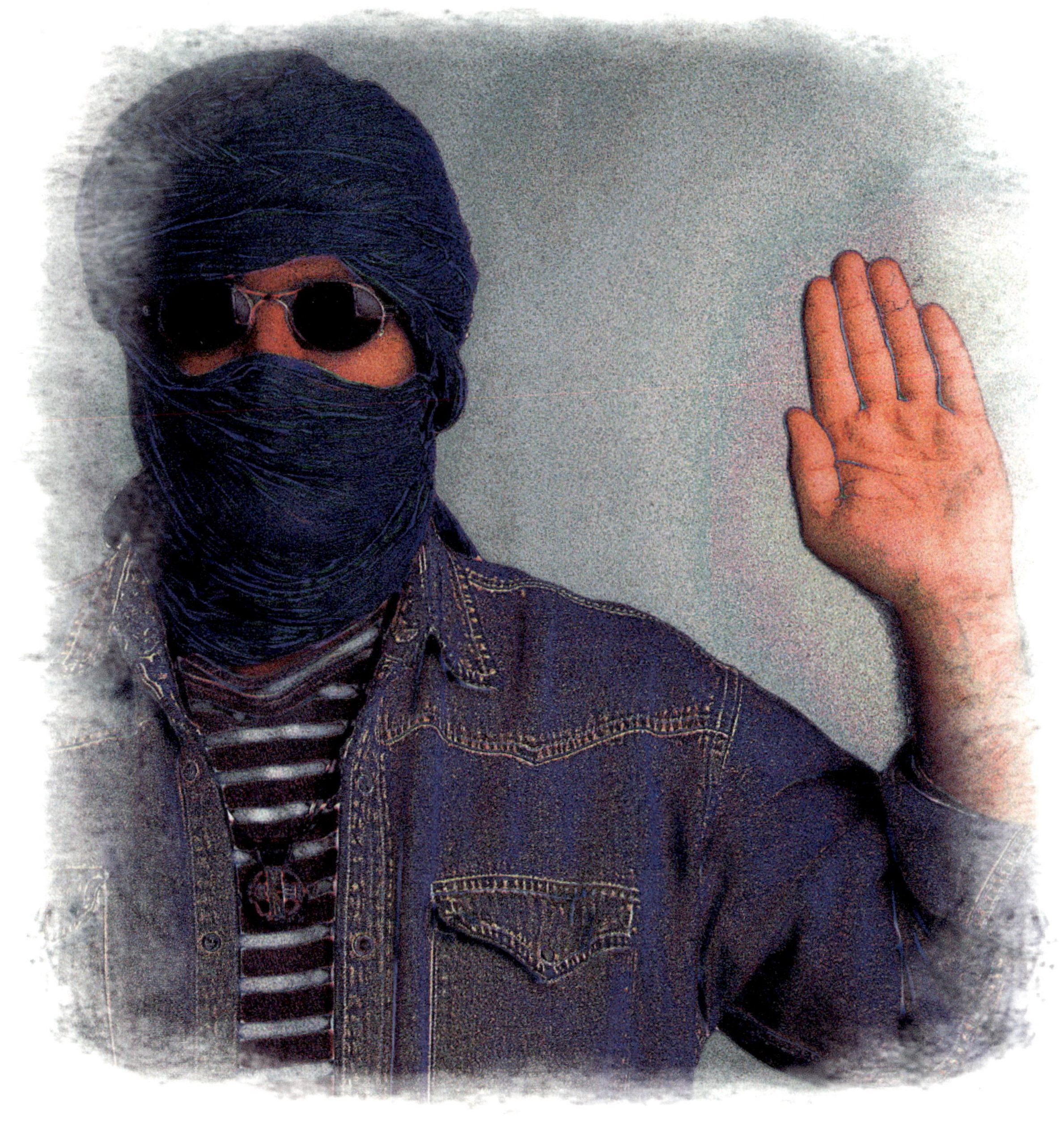

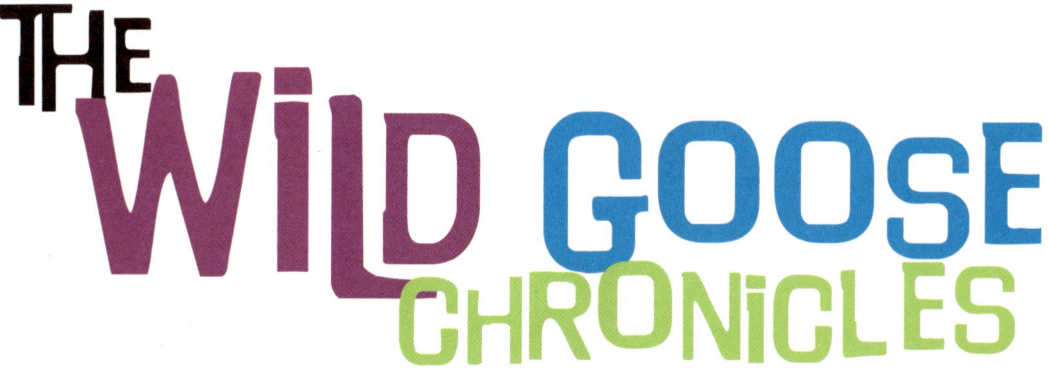

THE WILD GOOSE CHRONICLES

TRENT HARRIS

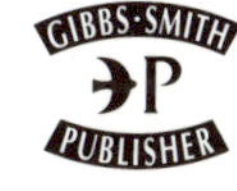

GIBBS·SMITH PUBLISHER

Salt Lake City

First edition
02 01 00 99 98 5 4 3 2 1

Published by
Gibbs Smith, Publisher
P.O. Box 667
Layton, Utah 84041
Orders: (800) 748-5439
Visit our Web site at www.gibbs-smith.com

Cover design by Ed Bateman and Trent Harris
Back cover design by Hally/O'Toole Design
Interior design by Trina Stahl

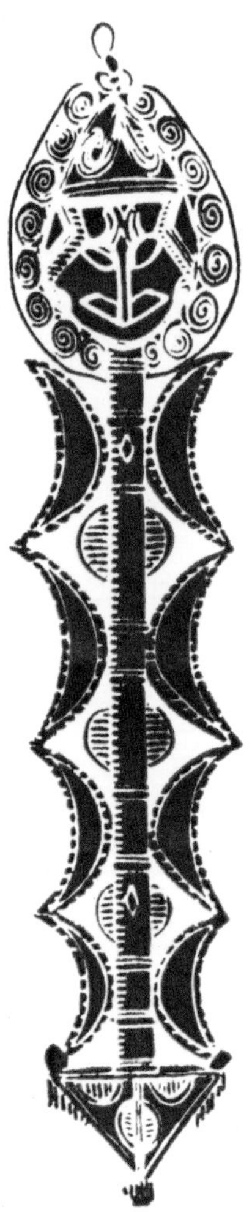

Printed and bound in Hong Kong

Library of Congress Cataloging-in-Publication
Data
Harris, Trent.
The wild goose chronicles / Trent Harris.
  — 1st ed.
        p. cm.
ISBN 0-89705-860-9
1. Tombouctou (Mali)—Description and travel.
2. Harris, Trent—Journeys—Mali—Tombouctou.
I. Title
DT551.9.T55H37 1998
916.623—dc21
                                    98-3452
                                    CIP

TO ANDREA

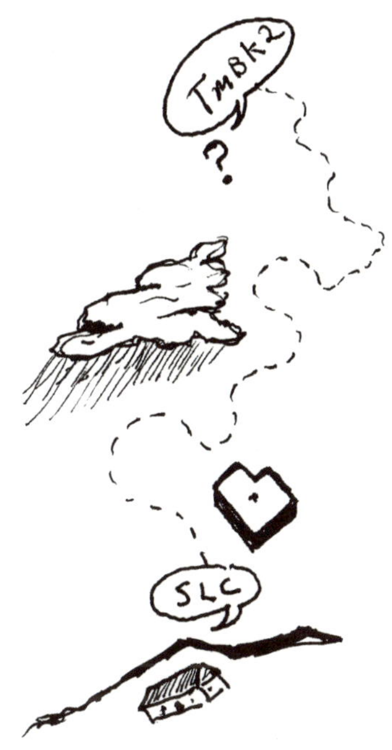

Tmbk2
?
SLC

CHAPTER 1

ATTACK OF THE FLABBERING BLABBERHOLES

It was 1992. People were against me. No one in L.A. would give me a job. No one would invite me to a party. Even my girlfriend had mysteriously transformed herself into an icy pit bull. Our relationship consisted of me jump-starting her car every other day, and on the odd occasion when she did climb into bed with me, she kept all her clothes on, including her boots. Yes, I was twenty years older than her, and yes, I was in a cranky mood. But I was not in the middle of a midlife crisis. I was in the grip of something far more powerful.

It was the week after the L.A. riots. My house had nearly been burned to the ground and my film *Rubin and Ed* had just been released.

Nobody went.

The city was in a particularly mean mood and a movie about two Republicans trying to bury a frozen cat just didn't seem to strike the right chord. The critics were in a mean mood too. They

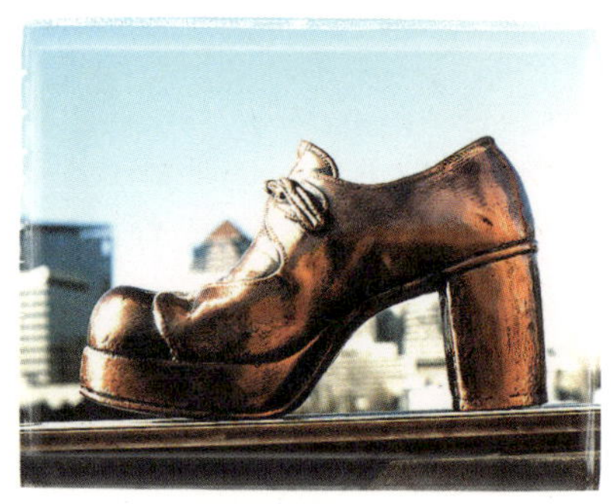

fell all over themselves trying to come up with the most horribly witty things to say about my film. One idiot, I think he was from the *Los Angeles Times,* said, "The kind of mind that would have Crispin Glover [the star of my film] suck on an **Odor Eater** should have his driver's license taken away." Another **doofus,** Jay Carr of the *Boston Globe,* said, "*Rubin and Ed* is easily the worst movie of the decade," and this from a man whom I'm sure **fantasizes** about Barbra Streisand **sitting on his face.**

To digress a bit here, I actually saw Barbra Streisand once. It was early on a Sunday morning in West L.A. She was driving a Jeep wagon. She was wearing a stocking cap pulled way down over her eyebrows. I watched from my car as Ms. Streisand stuck her index finger way up her famous nose. After what seemed like an eternity she removed her finger and examined something stuck to the end. She flipped the something out her window, and it landed on my windshield. Then she turned and looked right at me.

I didn't know what to do so I turned on my windshield wipers. She slammed her foot on the gas and went right through the red light.

I never saw Barbra again.

Anyway, back to the story . . .

It was 1992 and everybody was against me so I got up really early and placed a call to the U.S. embassy in Bamako, the capital of

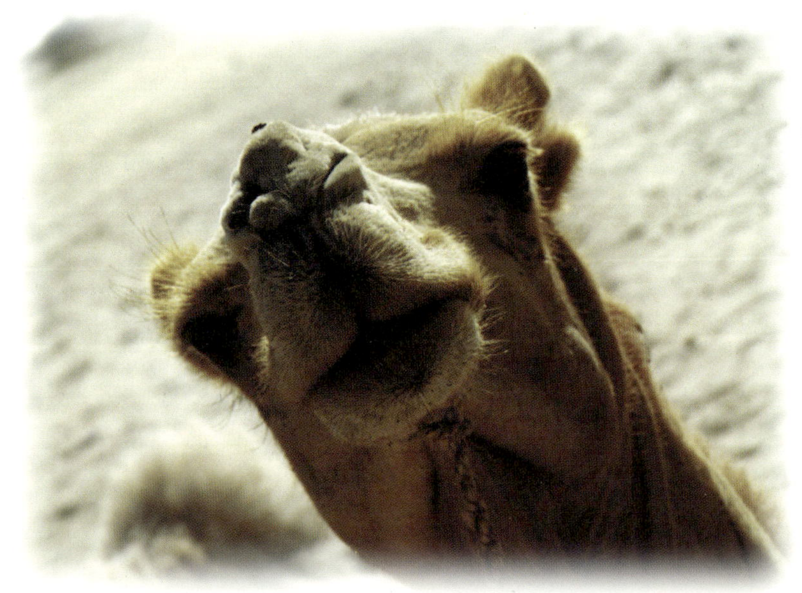

Mali. A girl with a remarkably **sexy** voice answered in French. I told her I wanted to take a boat from Mopti to Timbuktu and asked if there was enough water in the river. She came back in broken English saying, "Rebels . . . shooting . . . boat . . . rebels." I asked her if I could talk to an American, someone who spoke better English. She said, "No Americans at the American embassy." I said, "Why aren't there any Americans at the American embassy?" She hung up.

I called the State Department in Washington, D.C., to find out what in the hell was going on and got a recording. The message said, "Whatever you do, don't go to Mali because you'll probably get **killed."** I figured Mali had to be better than Hollywood so I went down to a travel agent to buy a ticket. The travel agent said, "In all good con- science I can't sell you a ticket to Mali because there are all kinds of travel warnings out and *I don't want your death coming back to haunt me."*

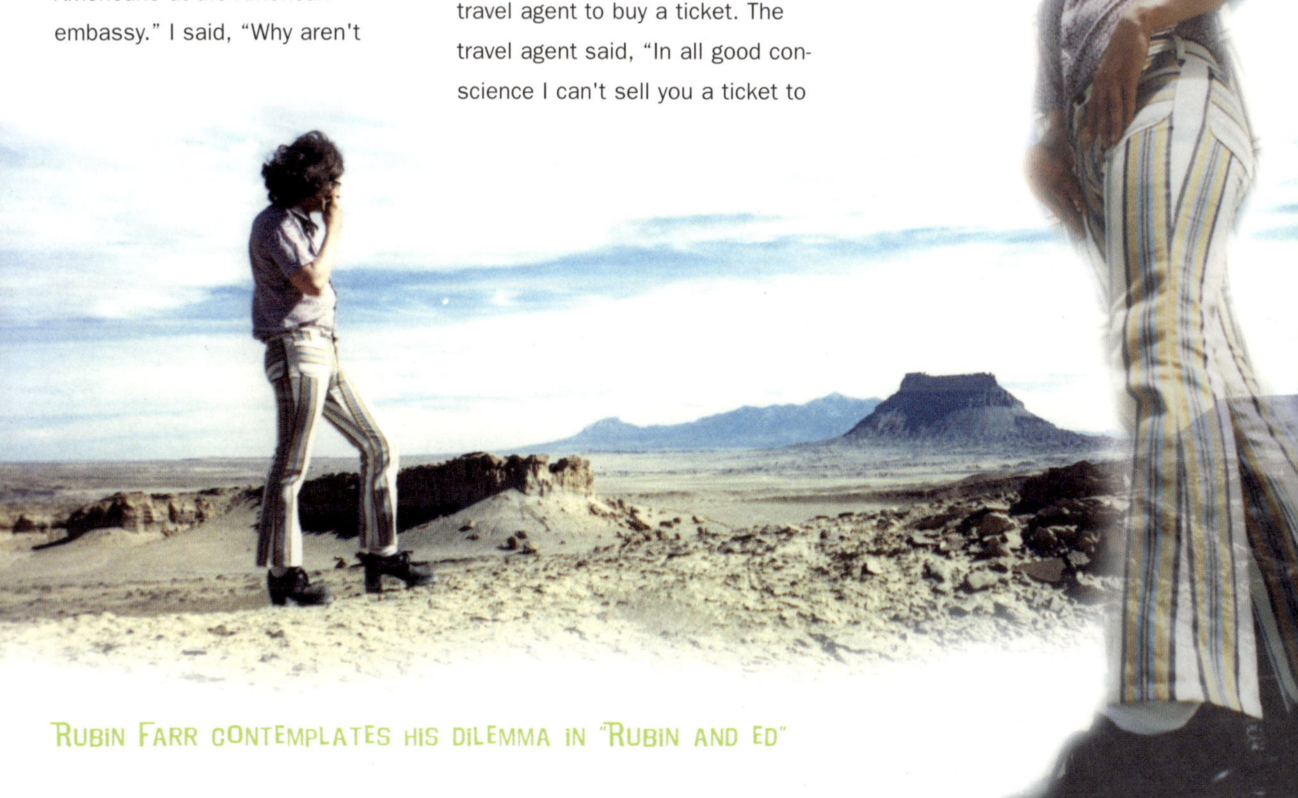

PLAN 10

A GOOSE AND A GIRL ARE NEVER SATISFIED.

TURKISH PROVERB

A BACHELOR AND A DOG
MAY DO EVERYTHING.

POLISH PROVERB

Timbuktu went on the back burner and I came up with another plan. Late one night **I loaded my dog in the car and left Hollywood.** I returned to my hometown, Salt Lake City, and immediately made another film, *Plan 10 from Outer Space.* This is a terrific movie, a **sci-fi epic about Mormons** that was ultimately banned in both

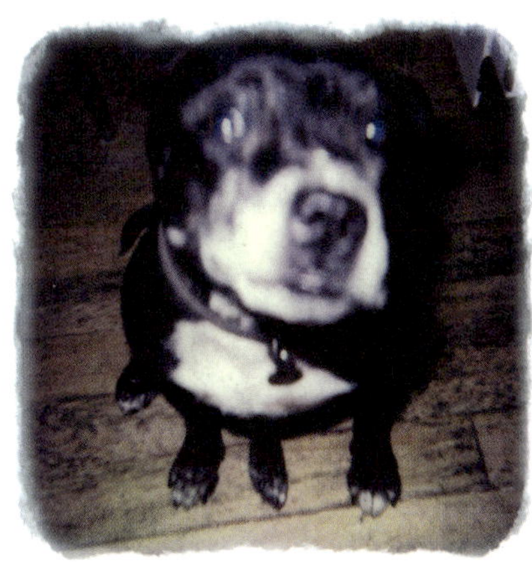

Boise and Pocatello, Idaho. During the filming I fell in love with a wonderful girl and things were going fine. Then, mysteriously, *that wonderful girl transformed herself into an icy pit bull.* Yes, I was twenty-two years older than her, and yes, I was really really cranky. But I was not, and I want to make this perfectly clear, in the middle of a **midlife crisis.** What I was experiencing was far more profound. I was possessed by an **evil** spirit, one with feathers and an orange beak.

To digress a bit here . . . I have known Scott for many years. Once I told him that I had had sex with a girl named Sandra on the swing set in Lindsey Gardens and that a good time was had by all. Scott got mad. It turned out he had also loved Sandra but he had never had the courage to have sex with her on the swing set in Lindsey Gardens. He called me a liar and a pervert. I told Scott I wasn't lying and that I had the pictures to prove it. Scott got really mad and stormed out of my office. Ten minutes later he came back and asked to see the photos. He looked at them for a while and then he slugged me in the eye.

5

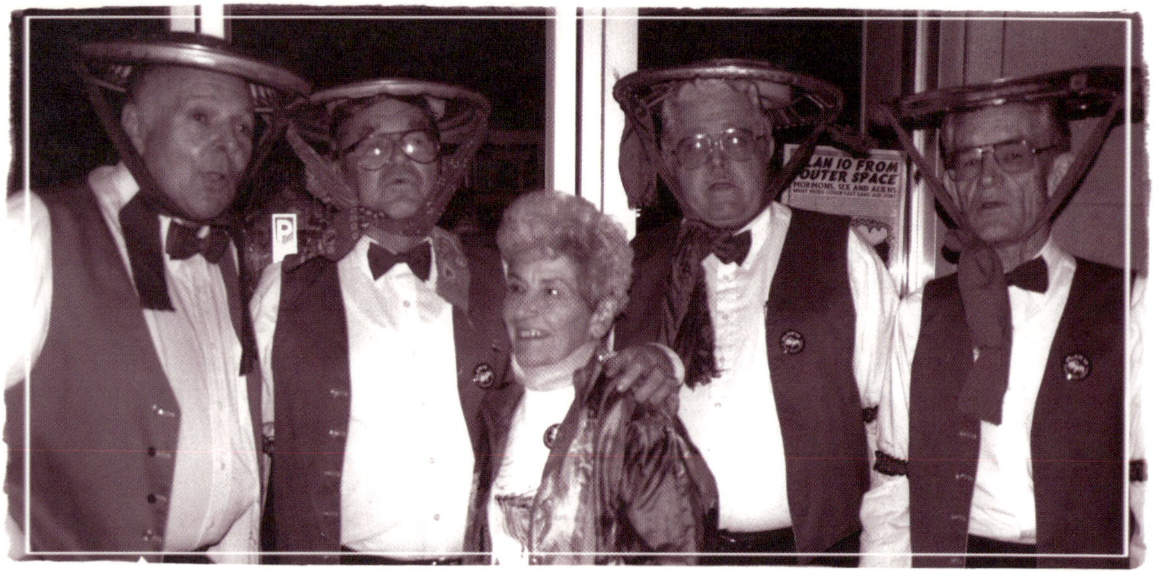

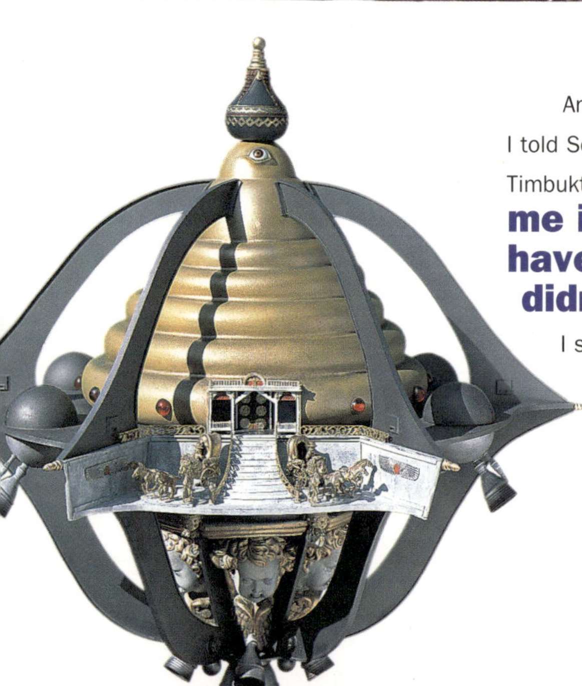

Anyway, back to the story . . .

I told Scott I was going to Timbuktu. **He asked me if he could have my TV set if I didn't come back.**

I said yes. Then he asked me why I was going.

"Because," I replied,

*"There's a wild goose honking in my ear—and the **bastard** won't shut up!"*

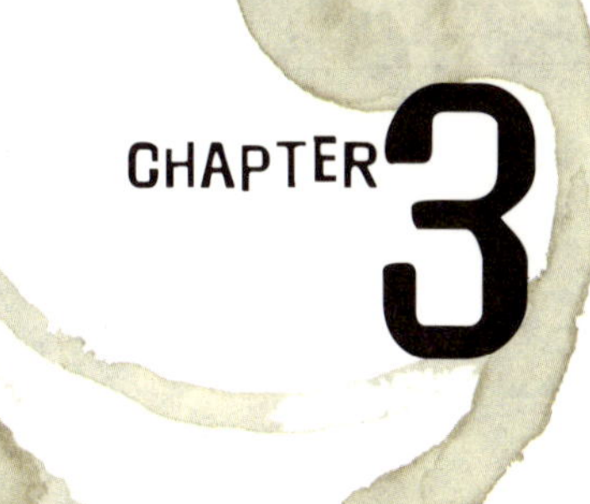

CHAPTER 3

MANY HAVE TRIED AND MANY HAVE DIED

"Who is this wild goose?" Evgeny asked. "I don't know," I said. "What does this goose want with you?" "I don't know that either," I said. Then Evgeny, who is from Russia, asked, "Trent, what does it mean to kiss your ass good-bye?" "It's a way of saying, get ready for trouble," I explained. "It's a way of saying, **doom is on the horizon.**" Evgeny thought for a moment, then handed me a couple of books and said, *"Trent, kiss your ass good-bye."*

The first book was about the Scottish explorer Gordon Laing, who set out for the fabled city of Timbuktu in July of 1825. Six months into his journey, somewhere in the middle of the Sahara, he was jumped by a band of desert pirates known as the **Blue People.** They stabbed Laing eight times in the head and once in the back of the neck, fractured his jaw, and split his ear. Then they shot him in the hip with a musket ball that went all the way into his back, stabbed him five more times in the right arm, **broke three** of his **fingers,** and slashed his wrist. Then the Blue People stabbed Laing three more times in the left arm, broke it, and then, **just to be mean,** stabbed him once in the right leg and once in the left.

Still Laing managed to **climb onto his camel** and struggle another 650 kilometers to the oasis of Sidi el Muktar,

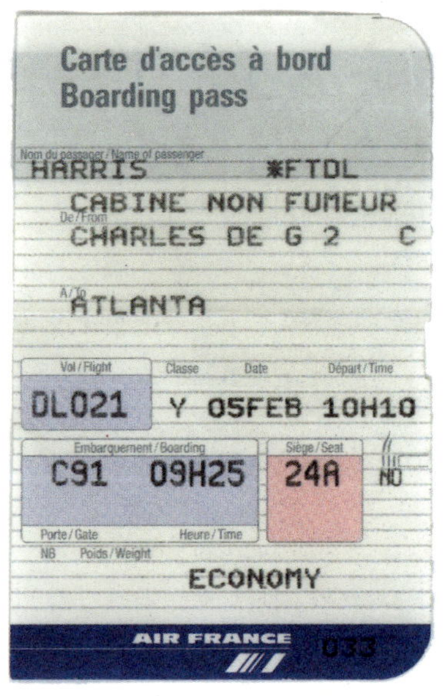

where he spent the next four months recuperating. Finally, on August 13, 1826, Laing became the first European to set foot on the sandy streets of Timbuktu. He spent five weeks there looking at **mud huts, eating goat, and swatting flies.** Then word came that the Fulani Sultan, who had recently laid claim to Timbuktu, didn't like Christians and wanted Laing dead. Laing loaded up his camel and headed back to Europe. His small caravan was attacked again. This time an agent for the Fulani Sultan finished what the Blue People had failed to do. Passersby **buried** Laing in a sand dune; then in 1910 **somebody dug him up** and returned his body to Timbuktu, where he still remains.

VOMIT RAIN AND OTHER WONDERS

Evgeny's other book was about Mungo Park, another Scottish explorer **also possessed by the goose** who, in 1795, set out to map the Niger River and along the way visit Timbuktu. He never made it to the city, but his journals are so **damned weird** I am going to talk about them here.

After only a few days in Africa, Mungo arrived at the **city of Kolar** in the **kingdom of Woolli** where he made note in his journal of a curious costume made of bark he found hanging in a tree. Natives told him that this was the costume of Mumbo Jumbo and that it was the custom in the kingdom of Woolli for a man to put on the suit of Mumbo Jumbo and call for a big party. At that party Mumbo Jumbo would **single out the bitchiest of his multiple wives, strip her naked** in front of the entire village, **tie her to a post,** and **prod her profusely** with his rod.

Mungo moved on to the village of Teesee. There he made note that the inhabitants **ate moles, rats, and squirrels**, but that the women of Teesee would never eat an egg. In fact the biggest offense

to a woman of Teesee was to say to her, "Hey, how would you like an egg?"

On Mungo went, into the land of the Moors, where the **women were very fat.** Mongo wrote this of these women,

"A perfect beauty is a load for a camel."

Then Mungo was kidnapped and taken to see Ali, Sheik of

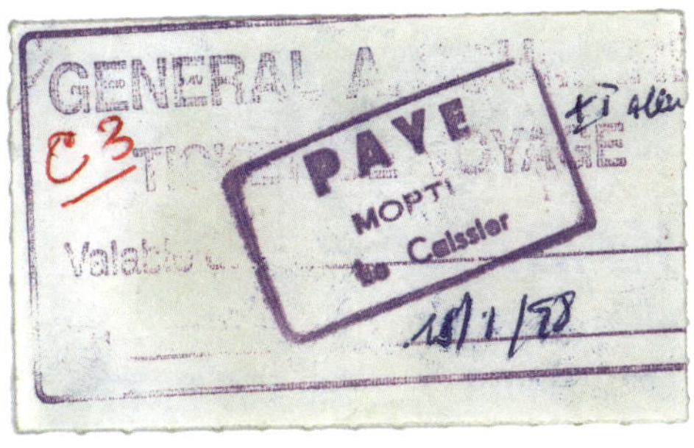

Ludamar, who also hated Christians. **The Sheik decided to pluck out Mungo's eyes,** but Mungo managed to escape and went back to England, where he regrouped, got forty soldiers, and headed back to finish mapping the Niger and find Timbuktu.

Due to delays, Mungo set off in the hot season, known for its **terrible hurricanes.** Then the expedition was overtaken by the rainy season, known for its **terrible rains.** "The rain had not commenced three minutes before many of the soldiers were **affected by vomiting;** others fell asleep as if **intoxicated."**

Then came the obligatory bouts with malaria and dysentery. By the time the expedition reached the Niger River there were only eleven men left and they **were a real mess.** But on they went, down the river, only to be **attacked by natives** with spears, arrows, and big rocks. Mungo finally leaped off his boat into the muddy, **hippo-infested** water and died a horrible death.

IF YOU KNEW WHY IT WAS MYSTERIOUS, THEN IT WOULDN'T BE MYSTERIOUS.

Everyone has heard of Timbuktu but no one is quite sure why. A few know the city for what it is, an ancient oasis on the white-hot southern edge of the Sahara, so far from anywhere that **even its inhabitants,** the Blue People, **don't know where it's at.** Rumor has it that these Blue People **are extremely cranky.**

This may be due to the fact that the summer sun of Timbuktu is **hot enough to bake their balls.** Or perhaps the Blue People are just embarrassed that their town is named after a woman with an extraordinarily big belly button. *Tim* means *well* in Tamacheck, and *Bouctou* was the name of an old woman that once guarded the well when the city was nothing but an oasis. Legend has it that this woman had a very large navel, hence *Timbouctou* to many means **"woman with a big belly button."** As for the Blue People, they are actually a tribe of fierce warriors known as the Tuareg, once notorious for raiding caravans that crossed the Sahara. The Tuareg wear clothes dyed with indigo. The **dye** tends to rub off on their skin, giving them the appearance of being blue, hence the nickname, the Blue People.

So, you're thinking, all this is **fascinating but so what?** Why is Timbuktu famous? For one reason and one reason only: it's just so **damned hard to get to.**

Scott asked me my travel plan. "First I will fly to **Bamako,**" I said, "which **means 'Crocodile River.'** From Crocodile River I will ride a moped to the city of Mopti and find the Bozo Bar. There I will have a beer and book passage on a pinasse (a big canoe) captained by a member of the **Bozo** tribe. My research has revealed that the Bozos are wise to the ways of the Niger River and often make money transporting adventurers such as myself. My Bozo captain will take me to Woman with a Big Belly Button where I will visit with the cranky Blue People. If all goes well, after a time I will continue down the river to the ancient city of Kaw Kaw (now called Gao) and attempt to talk to the King of Kaw Kaw and find out what is going on there. I shall then return to Salt Lake City and be **triumphant.**"

THE SMELL OF MONEY

A WATERMELON WILL NOT RIPEN IN YOUR ARMPIT.

ARMENIAN PROVERB

Truer words have never been spoken," I said. "But what is the **subtext** of this proverb? What are the Armenians trying to tell us? I hope to find the answer in Timbuktu." I blurted this out in a bar to a girl I was trying to impress. She didn't think it was funny. She asked me what kind of car I drove. I told her I owned a vintage 1978 Oldsmobile Omega that I called Hurdle, Hurdle the Blue Omega. She asked me how, if I didn't own a better car than that, I expected to finance my trip to Africa. I told her that indeed my foray into feature films had rendered me **penniless;** however, my years in Hollywood had left me with one untapped resource. I had in my possession an invitation to the 1985 Sean Penn/Madonna wedding. I also had a thank-you card signed by both. I told her I would sell these items and buy a plane ticket. She said that was a **stupid** idea.

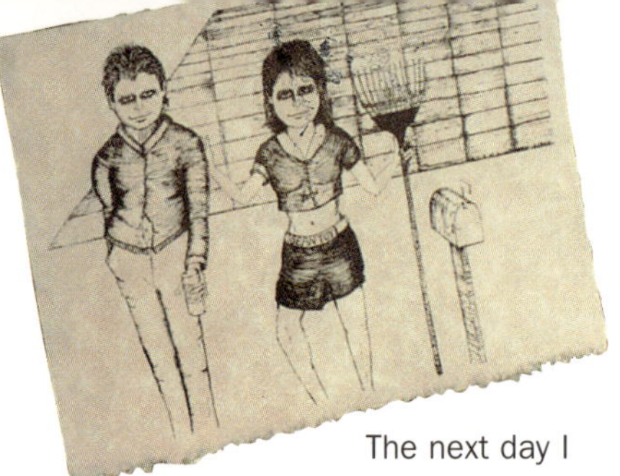

The next day I took the invite and thank-you card to my friend Ken Sanders, a dealer in **rare books** and documents. I told him he could have it for two grand. He took it on **consignment** instead.

IF YOU TAKE A WIFE FROM HELL, SHE WILL BRING YOU BACK.
AMERICAN PROVERB

One may wonder how the poor son of a **tractor dealer** from Idaho such as myself ended up at **Madonna's wedding.** It was 1981 and I was making a student video. I got Sean Penn's number from a friend, called him up, and offered him the lead. **Penn** took the part and completely **transformed himself** into the main character, Larry Huff, a young man **tormented** by his **compulsion** to dress like Olivia Newton-John. The video had some funny parts, but overall it was pretty disturbing—**Sean dressed in DRAG,** trying to sing like Olivia. In any case, when this video was finally shown at the American Film Institute it **scared the shit** out of most of the students and faculty. Penn and I hung around a bit, and a couple of years later he invited me to watch him get married.

I think everyone at the wedding, with the possible exception of Sean, knew the **marriage** was **doomed.** Most thought the couple would kill each other within a week. Much to Penn's credit, he made it a

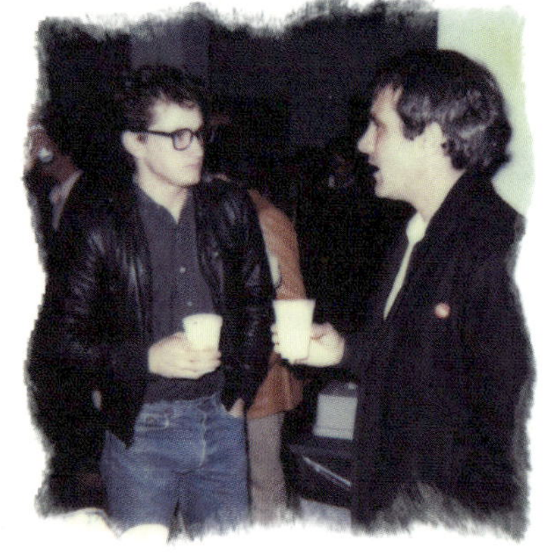

couple of years before the whole thing **melt**ed **down.** I asked him once what it was like being married to Madonna. He said he wasn't sure because he'd been **drunk** the entire time. In any case, I always liked Sean and I was grateful to him now for providing me with the means to buy a plane ticket to Timbuktu.

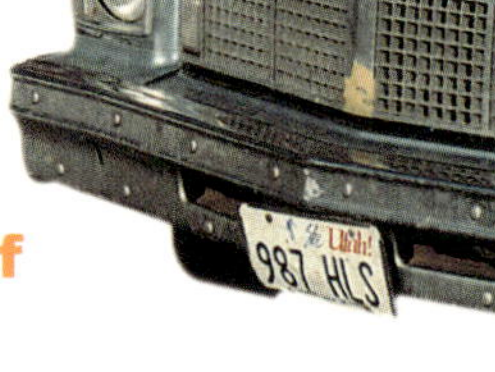

HOW TO SAY "THANK YOU" IN BAMBARA BEFORE YOU'RE KILLED

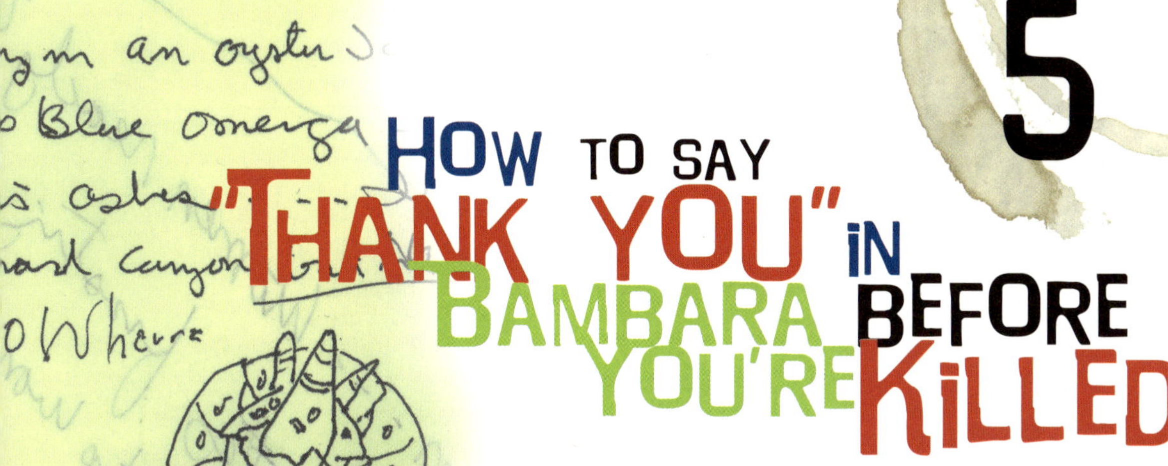

it became apparent to me that I had better get in shape for this trip. Numerous **vices** had left me out of breath, fat, and slow, so I joined a gym and enlisted the help of a trainer named Garth. After two weeks I had **pulled a groin muscle,** screwed up my shoulder, and was still out of breath, **fat,** and slow. Garth recommended I double my workout routine.

Meanwhile I continued my **research** into Mali. I went to the library and checked out an armload of books from which I discovered the average annual **rainfall** of Mali (not very much), the most popular crop (some say cotton), the population (about 9,000,000), and the president (Alpha Oumar Konaré). Then I went to the Internet, where I gleaned the following information:

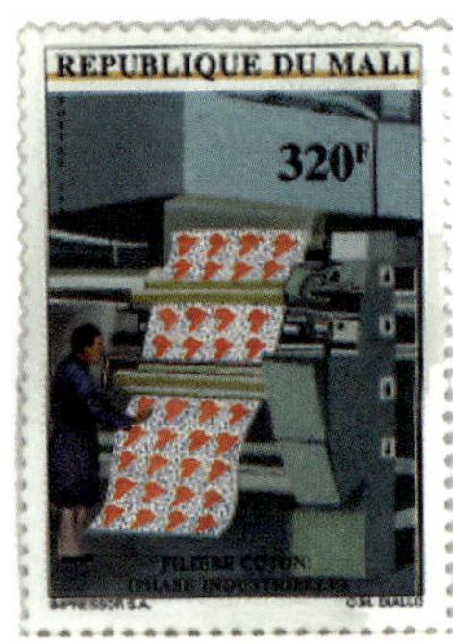

The U.S. Embassy in Bamako urges U.S. citizens to exercise caution while traveling in the north or to any isolated area within Mali. Banditry and, especially, carjacking persist.

Pickpocketing and armed robberies are common in downtown Bamako, along major travel routes, and around principal cities. Wise travelers stay alert, remain in groups, and avoid poorly lit areas after dark.

Security problems have forced the Peace Corps to forbid its volunteers to travel alone into Mopti as of June 1997.

Tuaregs attacked several towns around Timbuktu, **killing** almost one hundred people in one week. Due to **hard conflicts** north of the Niger River, boat travel has been delayed and domestic flights canceled. It is strongly recommended that any travel by land be done only in convoys.

Popular words and phrases in **Bambara,** a common language in Mali:

Good morning
e-nee-**SOH**-goh-mah

How are you?
e-koh-kay-nay-**WAH**

Thank you
e-nee-chay

Good-bye
khan-bee-ah-**FOH**

Please don't kill me
ick-a-dick-a-doo

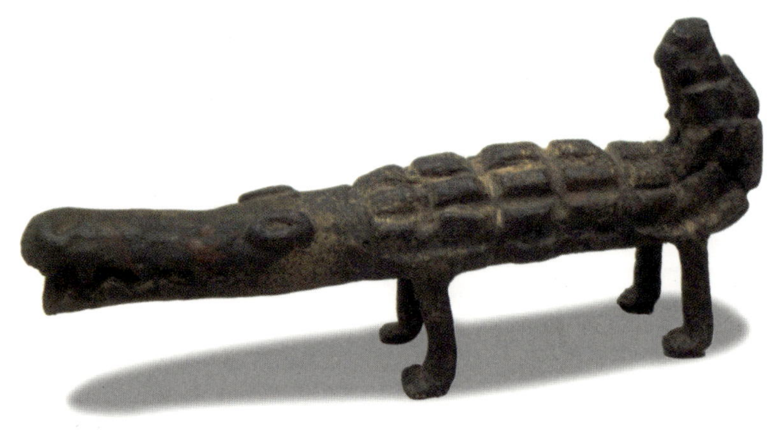

CHAPTER 6

BLASTO

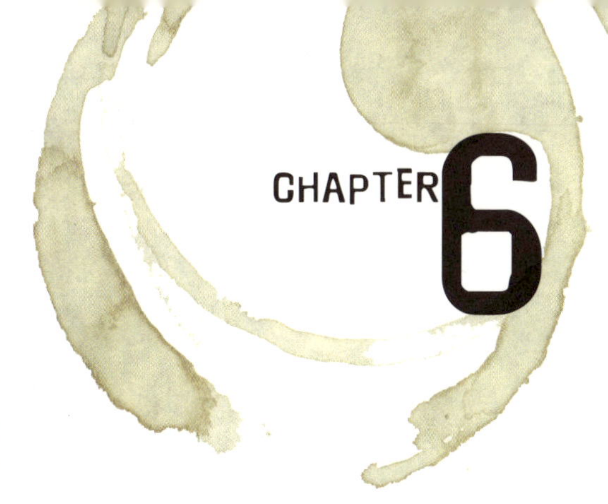

A GOOSE IS NOT A PIG'S COMRADE.
RUSSIAN PROVERB

I have thought long and hard about this proverb, and I don't have any idea what it means.

WHEN ONE GOOSE DRINKS, ALL DRINK.
GERMAN PROVERB

Now this proverb I understand. My friend Mike, who has traveled extensively in Africa, and I were drinking in a **bar called Juniors.** I was trying to work up the **courage** to get my travel

15

shots. He was going on about the ravages of yellow fever, malaria, **the plague,** cholera, and a dozen other **miserable diseases,** all of which are easy to catch in Mali. Then he told me about the most dreaded of all traveler's diseases: **BLASTO.** He said that when you get blasto the first thing that happens is your ears start flapping against your skull like screen doors in a hurricane. Then all the **blood** in your body **blasts** out your butt. In the final stages your brain turns to hot mush and you start cackling like a **frantic hyena** while you pee your pants.

There is no known cure.

Mike guzzled another beer and then told me about the time he had been **strip-searched** in some rinky-dink African frontier airport. The police had taken all his clothes into another room and left him standing buck **naked** in the hall for two hours. Mike had to give them $300 before he could get his pants back. That same day his camera and all his luggage were stolen.

Mike then ordered another pitcher and started **ranting** about **flies.** He hated flies more than anything. He said there are

billions of them in Africa and they get into everything, your hair, your food, your bed. And these flies have bright orange eyes that are as big as quarters. And they bite. Mike said he had been bitten on the chin by one of these flies and his entire head had swollen. He said he was unable to eat or talk for three days . . . then he said the mosquitos were even worse.

For a moment I considered stepping in front of a car; "Trent was going to Timbuktu but he was run over so now he can't go." The problem with that plan was that I had already bought my ticket and it was **nonrefundable.**

Mike said I looked too drunk to drive and offered me a ride to the clinic. **"Over my dead body!"** I screamed. "If I can't even drive to Timbuktu I sure as hell can't make it to the doctor!"

With that I left Juniors and went to get as many shots as possible. I took six in the arm. I was **sick as a cat** for eight days.

i HATE OPRAH WINFREY

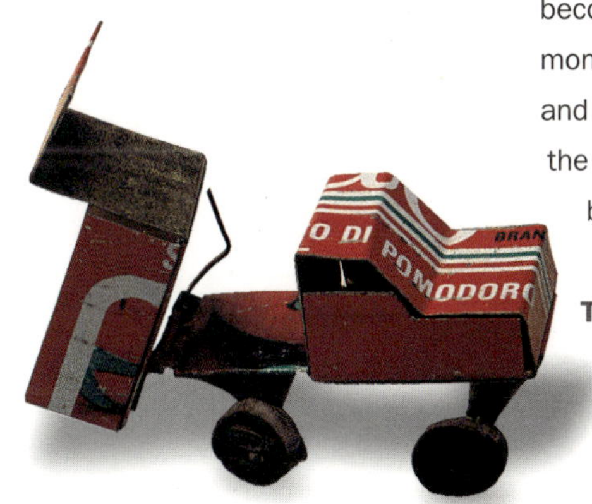

To be honest I was having serious **second thoughts** about my trip. My life had become quite comfortable in the month before my departure date, and the prospect of confronting the Tuaregs or, for that matter, blasto was losing its appeal. **Why was I going to Timbuktu?** People kept asking me that question and try as I would, I couldn't come up with a reason that **made any sense.**

Then, as so often happens in these kinds of situations, an answer came.

It happened when my friend Alex and I were discussing the importance of scary people, individuals who can **terrorize** the entire United States of America with nothing more than an idea.

For an idea to be truly terror- izing it must be:

1. fundamentally **true, and**

2. something the average person doesn't want **to hear.**

Alex and I came up with a list of **scary** people. Dr. Timothy Leary was a scary person, as were Allen **Ginsberg,** Martin Luther King Jr., **Brigham Young,** and Liberace. Alex then pointed out that all these people were dead. Neither of us could come up with one scary person who was alive today. Alex thought this might be a result of society's current lack of scary situations. There's **no Vietnam** so antiwar stuff is out. **Feminism** is hardly a radical notion anymore. Racial inequality isn't all that unequal,

and most of **today's rock and roll** **is totally limp.** So, the next question became, what would con- stitute a scary idea today? We couldn't think of one. Then we asked ourselves why. Alex thought it was **Oprah** Winfrey's **fault.** On her daily TV talk show Oprah answers all questions and puts everyone at ease, therefore rendering any revolution impos- sible. He went on to say that the biggest problem facing most Americans today is figuring out which video to rent.

Alex was right. Most people are reasonably com- fortable most of the time, and the last thing anyone wants is a scary idea.

This got me thinking. I had to admit that Oprah Winfrey had systematically ripped any sense of **foolhardiness, anarchy, and**

danger from our lives. I had to admit that she had answered all questions and that all we were left with was comfort. This thought made me uncomfortable.

It was at that moment that I realized why the wild goose was honking. The wild goose knows that when a man is faced with nothing but comfort, it is only a matter of time before that man goes berserk. The wild **goose** wasn't an **evil spirit** at all! The wild goose was my friend! The wild goose was forcing me to go to Timbuktu so that I could terrorize myself back to sanity! The **trip** was **on.**

LAST WILL AND TESTAMENT

My lawyer recommended I prepare the following document before my departure.

BEING OF SOUND MIND AND BODY I, TRENT HARRIS, DECLARE THIS MY LAST WILL AND TESTAMENT.

· I HEREBY LEAVE ALL MY FILMS TO THE SMITHSONIAN (PROVIDED THEY WANT THEM).

· MY STUFFED CAT, THISTLE, SHALL BE BEQUEATHED TO MY FRIEND GYLL HUFF.

· ANY MONEY FOUND IN MY COUCH GOES TO MY BROTHER JEFF.

· IF MY BODY IS EVER FOUND, PUT IT IN MY CAR, HURDLE. THEN TAKE HURDLE TO ONE OF THOSE CAR SQUASHERS AND SQUASH IT. TAKE THE REMAINS OF HURDLE AND ME TO THE DEEPEST PART OF THE GREAT SALT LAKE AND DROP US IN.

· AT MY WAKE I WANT THE SONG "I STARTED A JOKE" BY THE BEE GEES PLAYED THREE TIMES. IF ANYONE IS NOT CRYING AT THAT POINT, PLAY IT AGAIN.

SIGNED

____

DATE

____

WITNESSED BY

____

MY GOD . . . WHAT HAVE i DONE?

DO NOT SPEAK OF A RHINOCEROS IF THERE IS NO TREE NEARBY.

ZULU PROVERB

i got on a plane in Salt Lake City. Forty-eight hours later, in the middle of the night, the captain on Air Africa Flight 2508 announced we were about to land in Bamako. I felt the **plane bounce** onto the runway, then taxi to a stop. I looked out the window and spotted a few dim lights in the distance. I waited as long as I could, then got off the plane and wobbled through the inky blackness across the tarmac and into a small green room filled with fluorescent lights and soldiers. I presented my **passport** to a woman in a uniform behind a thick glass window. She **scrutinized** my documents and then **muttered something** in Bambara. I **stared** at her **blankly.**

She repeated herself, this time more forcefully.

"I'm an American," I whispered, "and I don't have a clue."

I reached for my passport and **she slapped my hand.** The woman eyed the puddle of **perspiration quivering** on the peak of my big red idiotic nose, then repeated her phrase again, this time in French. All the blood

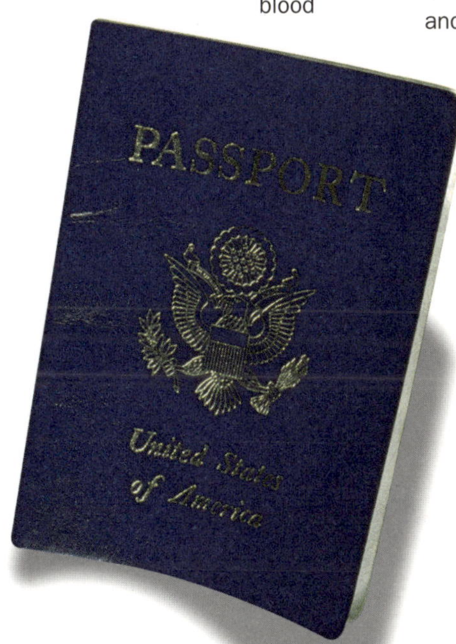

rushed to my head, and the room started to spin. I grabbed the counter with both hands to keep from falling and blurted out the only Bambara phrase I could think of: "Ick a dick a doo!"

The room fell silent.

Other puddles of perspiration rushed to join the one on my nose and together they waited.

Everyone waited.

I quickly scanned the room, searching for an avenue of **escape.** If I could bolt back to the plane, jump in, and lock the door, I might have enough time to figure out how to start the engines and fly to a **civilized** country where everyone spoke English.

Suddenly, from the sea of **puzzled black faces** emerged one that was white, **blindingly white.** Her hair was the color of sand and her eyes were sharp blue. She moved toward me and smiled. "What did you say to her?" she asked. "I think I said 'please don't kill me' but I'm not sure," I said. The white girl turned to the woman with my passport, smiled, and greeted her in Bambara. "She wants to know what hotel you are staying at," she said. "Oh!" I said. "Of course! The hotel! **I'm staying at the big hotel!** The really big hotel!"

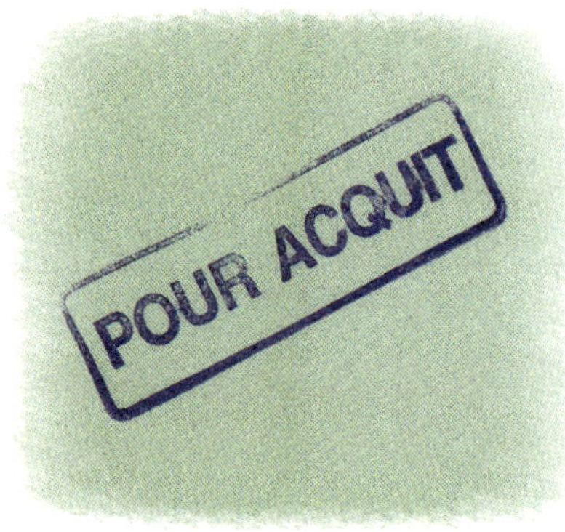

The white girl led me out of the green room and into the baggage-claim area. "Would you like to share a taxi?" she asked. I followed her **like a puppy** out of the terminal and into a dirt parking lot. She **bargained** with the drivers, threw my bag into the trunk of a small rattletrap Toyota, and off we went. Her name was Clover. She was

beautiful, twenty-six, and had been in Africa for two years working for **the Peace Corps.** She deposited me at the Hotel Le Grande and then **vanished** into the smoke-filled African night.

I purchased three **huge** bottles of beer from the hotel bar, went to my room, fastened the locks, and pushed a big chair up against the door. Then I took my knife out of my bag and placed it by the bed. I flipped on the TV and watched an old episode of *Speed Racer* dubbed in French. "Africa," I said to myself. "I've made it." I drank the beer and fell asleep.

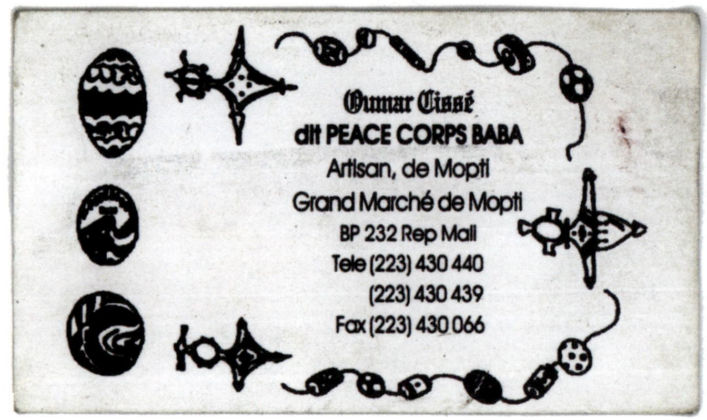

CHAPTER 10

I'M A VIRGIN!

IF RICE IS THROWN ON THE ROOF A THOUSAND CROWS WILL COME.

INDIAN PROVERB

The phone rang and I woke up. "Hello, Trent? This is Clover. Do you still want me to give you a tour of Bamako?" I pulled on my clothes and ran downstairs.

We walked out of the hotel into the **bright sun.** First I saw an African, then an African tree. I looked up at the white African sky and was so disoriented **I nearly fell down** the African steps. Drivers rushed forward beckoning us into their taxis. We declined. We passed through the hotel gate into the busy street and **began to wander.**

I walked. I stopped. I stared. It took me ten minutes to go ten steps. Everything smelled special. Everything looked **contrary.** The sounds were unthinkable, and my brain went into overdrive just trying to **suck** it all in. "What kind of bird is that? What does that sign say? **Look at that donkey's foot.** Do I eat this or wear it?" Clover answered all my questions. She said walking with me was fun because I was **still a virgin.**

Africa was new to me so I saw things, and that made her look at things too, things she'd long ago become accustomed to.

We went to the market, a crowded open-air **jumble** of stalls that sold everything from

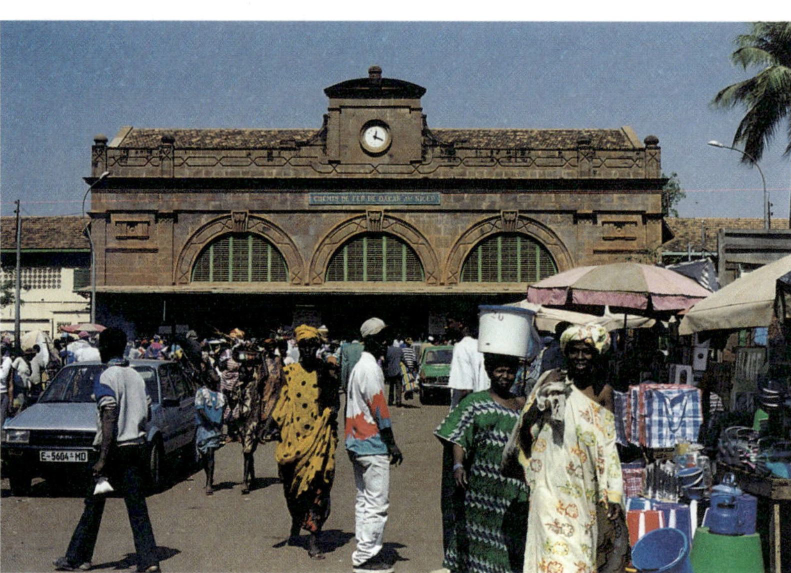

snakeskins to car parts. I tried on hats. I put things in my mouth. I bought a tiny bicycle made from sardine cans. Then we stopped at a **fetish** stall owned by a sorcerer. He sold all kinds of **animal parts,** some from endangered species. I asked him questions while Clover translated.

"What is that **monkey head** for?" "It is for the magic." "What about those bird beaks?" "They are for the magic too." "How about that green powder?" "It is magic powder."

Next we went to the post office to buy stamps, and two young black men approached us. "American?" one asked. I said yes. "Welcome to Bamako. My name is Bill Cosby and my brother is **John Travolta."** Cosby and Travolta wanted to be our guides. Clover politely brushed them off in Bambara and we continued on. Next we met **Mike Tyson,** who also wanted to be our guide, then Karl Malone, then Tupac Shakur. I asked **Tupac** if he knew Michael Jackson and he said no. (Africans often take on American names, and I'm not sure why. They also give foreigners African names, probably for the same reason.)

After hours of walking we purchased something Clover called **God in a bag,** a delicious frozen juice that made my mouth **bright red.** Then we made plans to meet later for dinner.

About 7 P.M. I climbed into a **burned-out shell of a taxicab.** There were no door handles and only springs to sit on. I paid about three dollars for the ride from my hotel to the Campanard, a kind of American oasis located in a relatively prosperous neighborhood in Bamako. I later found out the fare I had paid was triple the going rate.

I found Clover sitting with a young Arab man who worked at the Moroccan Embassy. He seemed surprised to see me. I ordered an **expensive** bottle of **French wine** and drank most of it. We all ate dinner, then Clover recommended that we head over to a nearby club to listen to African music.

The club, which was basically a courtyard surrounded by mud walls, was jammed. I found a corner and ordered another beer. Clover and the Moroccan disappeared in the crowd. I stood there, listening to the music and watching a beautiful black woman dressed in **skintight** red satin **dancing with a dwarf.** The Moroccan came back. He said he would soon move to the States. He said Clover would be much happier in the States too. He said she was a wonderful girl and that Mali was a stupid country and that he didn't like the music. Then he asked me where Clover was.

I shrugged.

He got upset and walked away.

To digress again . . .
When I was twenty-three I had a crush on a girl who was almost as attractive as Clover. One day I took her for a ride on my motorcycle and then back to my apartment so she could use my phone. She made her call and left a message with someone. Then she told me the motorcycle ride had given her a chill and she wanted to take a hot bath. She went into my bathroom, took off all her clothes, and then said, "When my husband calls, tell him I'm in the tub." I remember staring at her long beautiful legs and visualizing a bear trap. Anyway, I was having some of those same bear-trap feelings when I headed for the exit of the African nightclub.

Just as I reached the door Clover appeared. I told her I was leaving and she said she was ready to go too. I asked her where Mr. Morocco was and she said she didn't know.

We found a cab. Clover recommended that I sit in the front seat and she sit in the back. I said no and climbed in the backseat with her. When we reached the place she was staying, I told her I was heading for Timbuktu soon and thanked her for all her help. She told me that her term in the Peace Corps was just about up and that she would spend a few more weeks in Bamako and then go to a small village in the south where she really lived. There she would say good-bye to her host family and then head back to the States. She asked if I would like to come with her to her village. She explained that it would be a wonderful opportunity for me to see what Africa was really like.

What is wrong with this picture, I thought to myself.

This girl is way too pretty and smart to need me for anything. And besides, I wasn't there to chase women. I was there to . . . suddenly I couldn't remember why I was there.

Anthropologists have studied this phenomenon and have come up with a theory about why men act strange in situations of this type. The theory goes like this: Men are animals and are attracted to females with supple figures and bright eyes, capable of bearing them strong children. God knows what women are attracted to. Now, when a man spots an attractive woman his heart pumps all the blood from his head to his groin, and rational thought becomes impossible. Then his brain is subjected to a massive blast of endorphins and dopamine, causing strange feelings of euphoria and giddiness. Men are extremely vulnerable in this state. Even the smallest gesture on the woman's part can take on great significance. The way she picks up a saltshaker or wrinkles her nose can be interpreted as a come-on or a snub. At this point men often make decisions or say things that they will later regret.

"Listen, Clover," I began, "what you have to understand is that I haven't come halfway around the world just to . . . to . . . to . . . not see what Africa is really like. I need to see what Africa is really like in the worst sort of way. You cannot believe how much I have always wanted to see what Africa is really really like." She smiled, and we made plans to meet in a couple of weeks. I shook her hand and said good night.

RANDAL WAS A MORMON

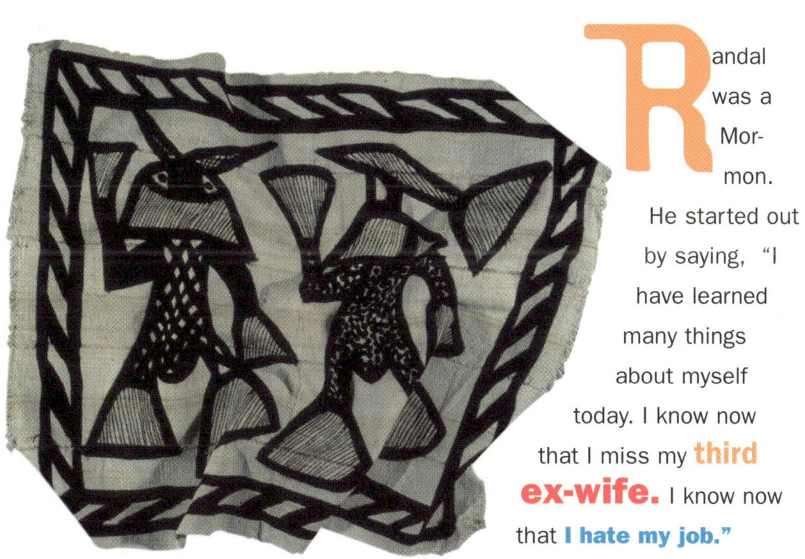

Randal was a Mormon. He started out by saying, "I have learned many things about myself today. I know now that I miss my **third ex-wife.** I know now that **I hate my job."**

Randal was sitting next to me on a bus **crammed** full of people bouncing down a bumpy road heading toward the city of Mopti. Randal went on. "I know now that I am very fortunate to have what I have. And I know now that **personal hygiene** is very important." Randal had been in Africa for two days, and travel was having a **profound** effect on

27

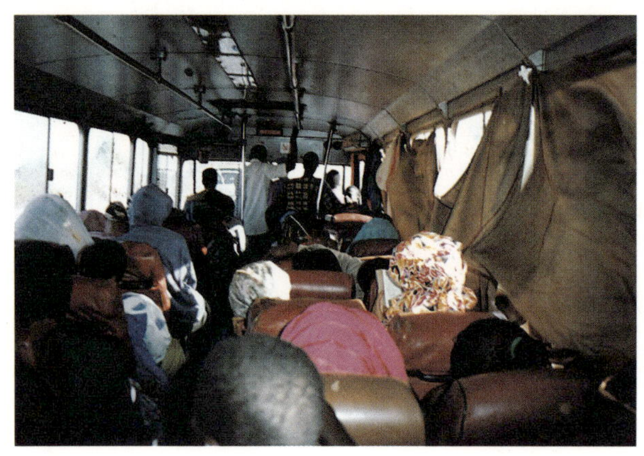

him. He told me that he had spent two years as a missionary for the **Mormons in Guatemala,** and that while there he'd become quite proficient at performing exorcisms. I asked Randal about the **exorcisms.** I too had been raised a Mormon, and I'd never heard of such a thing. Randal said that wasn't surprising because **Mormons really didn't do exorcisms.** "But," he said, "if you're in the middle of the boonies and somebody's full of the **Devil** and there are no

Catholics around, what are you going to do?" Somewhere along the line Randal had left the Church, **become a psychologist,** got married a few times, and **fathered a lot of children.** This was the first time in twelve years that Randal had been away from his home in Cleveland.

The bus stopped for lunch in the town of Segou, and we all got out. Randal opened up his backpack, pulled out a handful of T-shirts, **and began giving them to complete strangers.** I bought something I thought was **beef on a stick** and tried to eat it. We got back on the bus and took off.

Randal gazed through the window at the trees whizzing by.

"I know now that time is a funny thing," he said. "I know now that there is more in store for me than I ever imagined."

Six hours later we arrived in the ancient port city of Mopti. It was late. Randal and I decided to share a room.

We checked in to an African version of a road-side motel, then walked outside to the patio for dinner. Something whizzed by our heads and we looked up. "Giant parrots!" **Randal screamed.** There were thousands of them dive-bombing the courtyard, as big as geese, with faces like rats

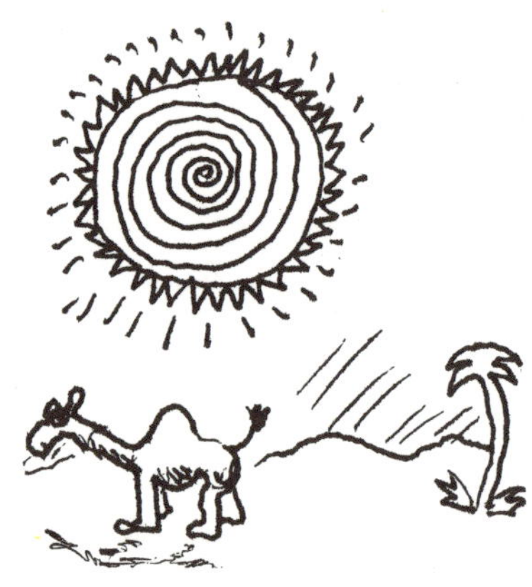

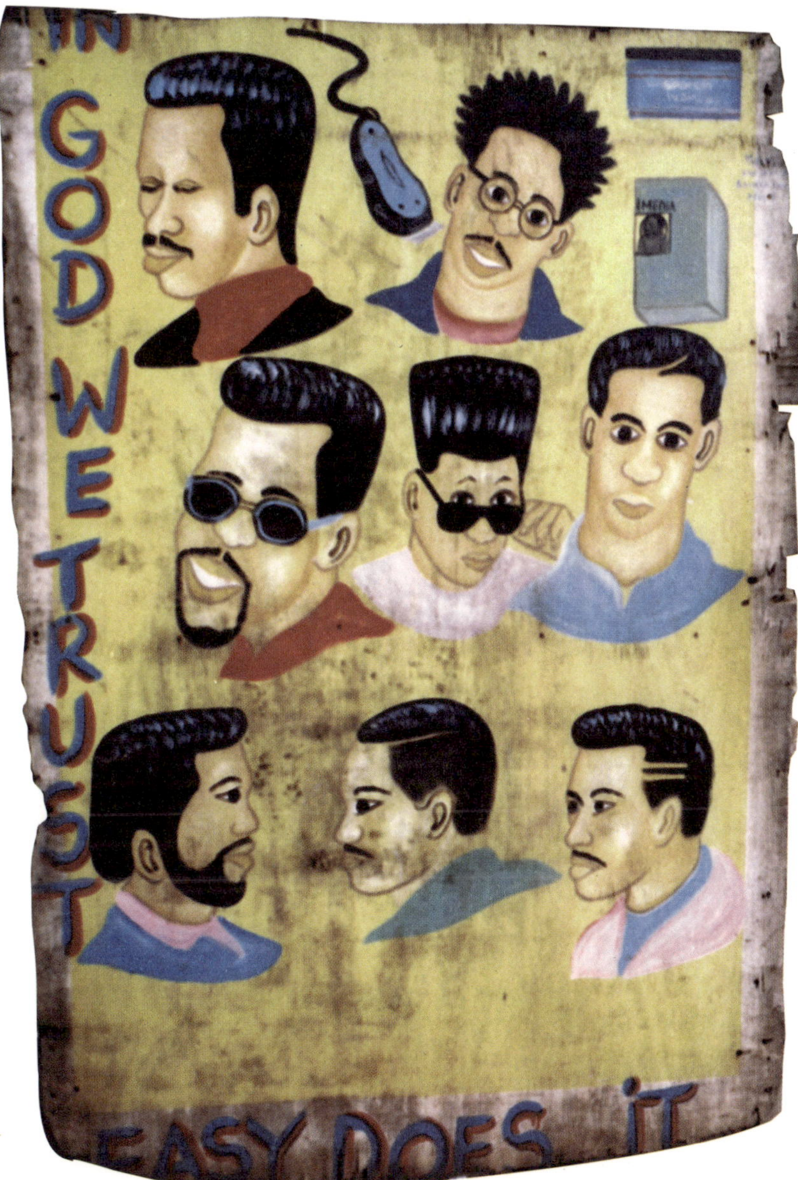

BARBERSHOP SIGN IN BAMAKO

and huge **furry feet** with hooks on the end. I pushed Randal under an umbrella. "Maybe we should eat inside," he said. "Are you crazy?" I said. "Look at those buggers! **You ain't going to see anything like that in Cleveland!"**

The waiter brought something to our table that looked suspiciously like a giant parrot. "What is this?" Randal said. "Chicken," said the waiter, then he hurried away. Randal said he didn't think he could eat it. I **tried to cut mine with a knife** but soon gave up. "Let's get some beer," I said. "No, thank you. I don't drink," said Randal. "Come on, man! One beer," I said, and I got up to get the waiter.

When I came back Randal was trying to take pictures of the parrots with his tiny flash camera. He drank one beer, then another, then another. **"Man oh man,"** Randal bellowed, "we're in the thick of it now!" "That's right!" I said. "We're in Africa!" Then Randal put a *Psychology Today* magazine on his head and stood up. **"Scat hat!"** he proclaimed, pointing at his head. Then he went over by a tree and started throwing **bits of bread** into the air. "Take my picture," he commanded. "Get those **fucking parrots** in there!" I tried, but his flash didn't work. Then Randal said, "Let's get some more beer!" and so we did.

"I know now that I am a new man," stated Randal.

"I know now that I will travel forever!"

The morning sun **screamed** through the giant-**parrot-**

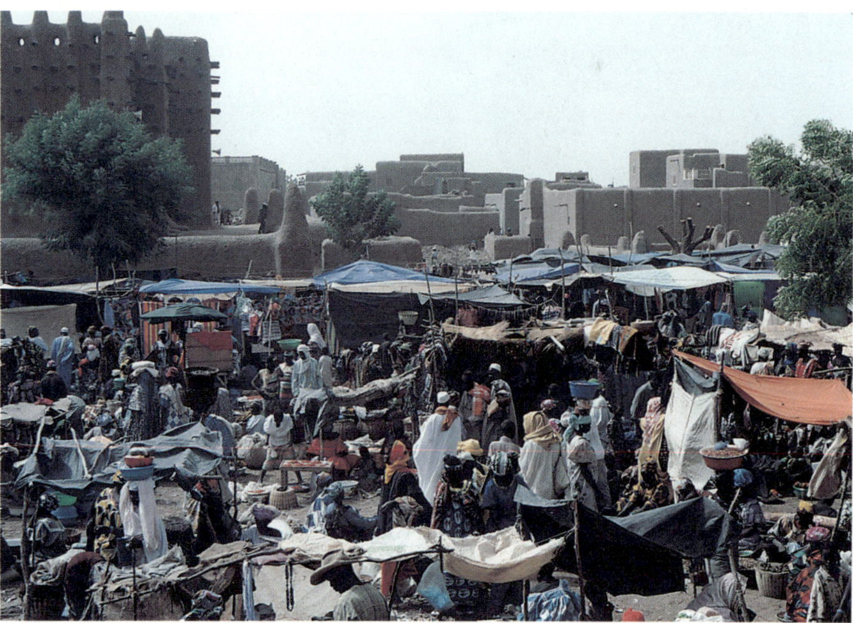

filled sky like a **big ripe basketball.**

Randal and I found a guide named **Baru** and headed into town. (One word about guides: Many travel books will say you don't need them. **Bullshit.** A guide can answer many questions, show you where the **toilets** are, and, most importantly, keep you from being mobbed by a bil-lion other guides, all asking you if you want a guide. Get one. Pay him well. You won't regret it.)

Now . . . Mopti is situated where the Bani and Niger Rivers meet. Near the center of town is the medieval market jammed with Fulani and Dogon natives, all wearing funny hats and busy buy-ing dried fish, strange fruits, and hunks of **raw meat covered with flies.**

There I watched men in turbans whip donkeys, saw chickens run for their lives, and found **goats** wandering around **eating rocks** and cans. I saw vendors hawking huge slabs of salt mined deep in the Sahara, along with plastic doohickeys, **monkey paws,** cigarettes, and Coca-Cola.

As we poked around I realized that Randal and I stuck out like two big white sore thumbs. People stared, some pointed, but without exception everyone was very friendly.

I would like to clear up a few things here . . .

First, the insects in Idaho are a hell of a lot bigger and a thousand times more voracious than any I encountered on my journey in Africa.

Second, I have never met a more friendly, civilized bunch of folks in my life. In fact, I felt a lot safer in Mali than I do in **Washington, D.C., or Salt Lake City for that matter.**

I asked Baru about the possibility of catching a boat from Mopti to Kabara, the port on the Niger River nearest to Timbuktu. He informed me that the river was now too low and that I had just missed the last passenger boat of the season. He said I could still book passage on one of the big canoes, but it was hard travel and he didn't recommend it for a tortoise such as myself. I corrected Baru. "*Tourist,* Baru, not tortoise. A tortoise is a turtle." Baru eyed me suspiciously and then said, "I still do not recommend it."

I asked Baru if he knew where the **Bozo Bar** was, and he pointed across the bay at a small building perched on a hill. I looked around for Randal and spotted him down by the shore of the river. He was engrossed in distributing more T-shirts. Dozens of people surrounded him. I heard him say, **"All gone! No more!"** but the crowd just kept getting bigger. I watched Randal open up his bag and start handing out other stuff: fingernail clippers, socks, CDs. Baru headed over, grabbed Randal by the arm, and dispersed the crowd.

We **ordered beers** at the Bozo Bar and sat down to make a plan. It turned out Baru was a Dogon (at least he said he was), and he claimed to know Dogon country like the back of his head. "Like the back of your hand Baru, not your head, your hand." Baru looked annoyed. Then he said, "You lie like a door!" Anyway, for an **exorbitant** price Baru agreed to lead Randal and me into **deepest, darkest** Dogon country. It meant several days of walking, and postponing my attack on Timbuktu, but for an adventurer such as myself the prospect of visiting this isolated, primitive tribe proved overwhelming.

Randal **gave his sunglasses to the waiter and we left.**

CHAPTER 12

THE KNIFE MY BROTHER GAVE ME

The next morning we took a cab to the market to buy supplies for the journey into Dogon country. I was hungry so I purchased a **cucumber,** pulled out my new knife, and cut off the end. I noticed something red on the cucumber and then realized that **I had just sliced off a big chunk of my thumb. Blood** was gushing all over the place. Randal yanked my medical kit from my bag and handed me the antiseptic. My hands were shaking so hard I **squirted** it all over the hood of the car. A crowd began to gather. People started yelling and handing me things, none of which I wanted to put on my thumb. I had to do something, so I stuck my thumb in my mouth. The **blood oozed** out, **down my chin** and all over the front of my shirt. I panicked. Images of horrible infections and amputations filled my head. I grabbed a bottle of whiskey from a stall nearby. "No!" screamed Baru, but it was too late. I poured the liquid on my thumb. It wasn't whiskey at all. **It was gasoline.**

The pain was un-**fucking-believable.** I grabbed my bloody knife and stabbed my water bottle. I doused my thumb, kicked off my shoe, **pulled off my sock,** and wrapped it around the wound. It worked. The bleeding slowed. I thrust my bloody fist into the air and yelled, **"No problem!" Everyone cheered.**

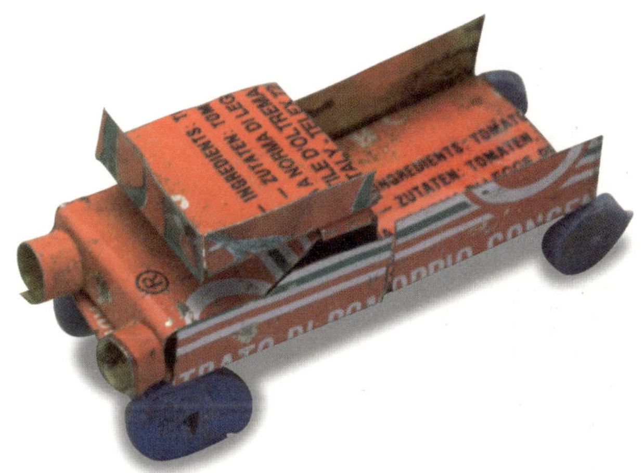

TERMITE CLITORIS

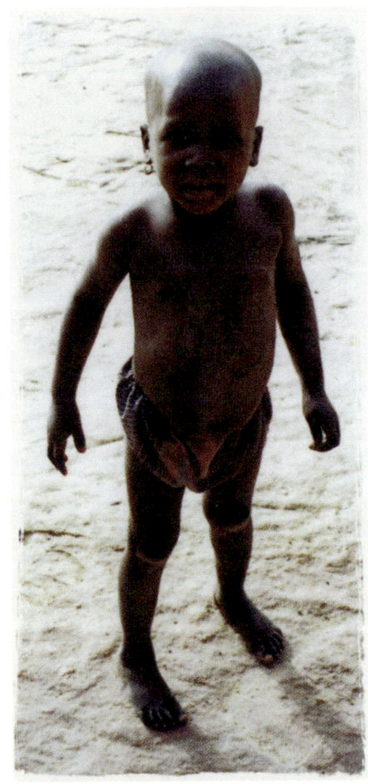

AN ITTY BITTY DOGON

We hired a car and driver to transport us to the edge of Dogon country. The **first part** of the road **was hellish,** then it **got worse.** The dust and potholes became rocks and thickets and then **the road vanished** all together. Eventually we emerged onto something that resembled a **cow path.** At that point we were stopped by a roadblock. Soldiers came to the car, **took our passports,** then disappeared into a grass hut. Randal and I sweated in the car while Baru and the driver went to straighten things out. There is something about being stripped of my passport that makes me really nervous. **"I would rather be without my pants** than my passport," I said.

Randal tried to change the subject. "So . . . " he said, "what do you know about the Dogon anyway?" "All I really know," I said, "is that they believe in a single god, Amma. Amma created the earth by throwing a ball of clay into space. **The ball took on the shape of a woman** with an **anthole for her vagina** and a **termite mound for her clitoris."** "Why are you trying to frighten me?" asked Randal. "I'm not. It's true," I said. "Now, Amma had sex with the earth, and **a jackal was born.** Then the jackal **raped the earth** and after that Amma didn't want to have sex with her anymore so he created two people from clay. But each of these people had both male and female sex **organs."** "Oh, **for hell's sakes,"** said Randal. "I tell you, it's true," I said. "I read it in this guide book," and I showed him the book and went on.

"Realizing that this sex-organ thing could be a big problem, Amma performed some kind of weird **circumcision** so the couple could have children. The kids didn't get along.

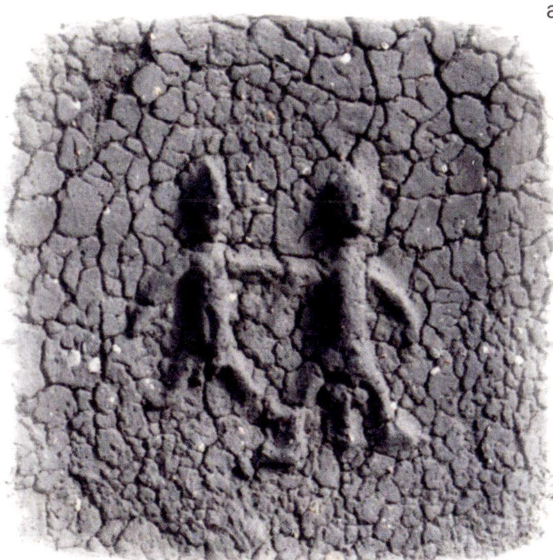

One stole language, and a couple of them had to be sacrificed." Randal seemed upset by this. "I don't think that's right," **he snarled.** "I would never sacrifice my children." "Right," I said. "Now this is the best part. Sigui is the biggest ceremony for the Dogon and they celebrate it only once every sixty years. The exact date of the celebration is calculated by figuring the periodicity of an invisible satellite that orbits the **Dog Star, Sirius."** This idea seemed to affect Randal. He sat silently for a moment and then said, **"Wow . . . and I thought my religion was weird."**

Then he looked out the window and turned pale. **"Are these soldiers going to kill us?"** he said. I looked over at the hut where Baru stood with his **hands in the air.** "My God," I said. "Are the keys in the car?" "Nope," said Randal. Then Baru put down his hands and went into the hut. Randal moaned, **"Oh shit!** What

motioned for me to be quiet, then went back inside. A minute later he and the driver came out. They got in the car with our passports. Baru was **furious.** The soldiers had **squeezed him** for money and got it.

Another hour of driving

gave him some kola nuts, and asked him if we could look around. The chief said yes.

In the center of Djiguibombo was a large, peculiar-looking tree. Baru said it was a baobab tree and very important to the Dogon.

"We use it

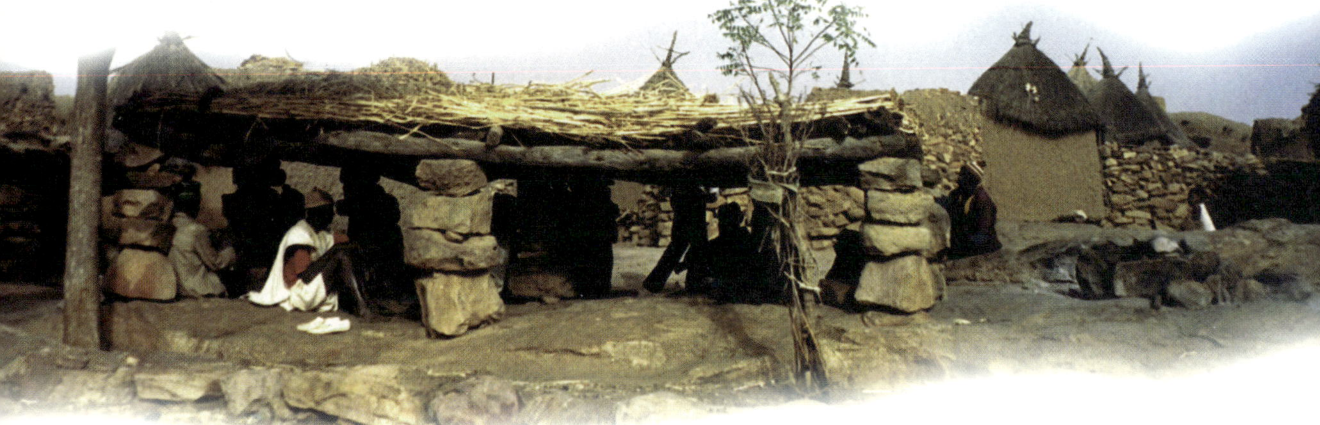

to make rope and eat its fruit," he said. He also said the **Devil had turned all bao-babs upside down so their roots would stick in the air.** I studied the tree for a moment. It did look like it was

are we going to do!?" I reached over and started **blasting** the horn. "Don't do that!" **he screamed.** Baru came out of the hut,

and we finally came to the **end of the road.** From there we began to walk.

The first village we came upon was called Djiguibombo [pro-nounced *dig-ee-jig-ee-boom-boo*]. Baru found the chief of the village,

upside down. Next we found a bizarre hut with no walls and a fat roof. Baru informed me that this was the hut of men and that no women were allowed. I inquired as to why **the roof was only about three feet** *off the ground.*

He explained that the roof was low so that if a man got mad while inside, he could not stand up,

from his pack to the people in the village. **Then he disappeared.**

When Randal came back he asked Baru if he had a coat hanger. Baru wasn't sure what a coat hanger was,

hence a fight was avoided. I sat in the hut and found it quite enjoyable. Randal stood outside distributing more stuff

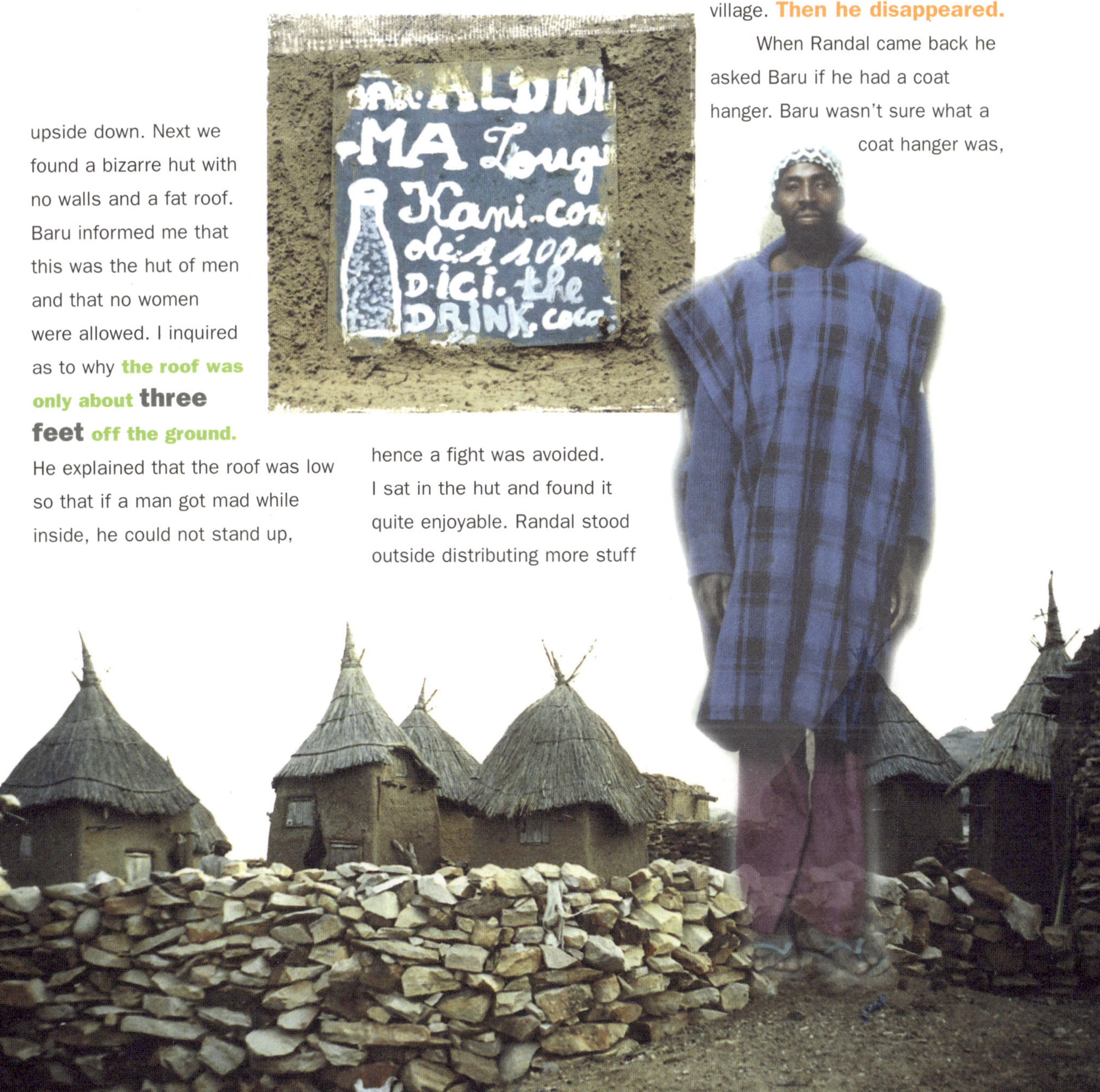

so Randal drew a picture of one in the dirt. Baru said, **"No,** I do not have a **coat hanger.**" I asked Randal what was up and he told me **he'd dropped his wallet while going to the bathroom.**

(A warning here: Using a third-world toilet is kind of like backing a dump truck up to a hole

VARMINTS ON A DOGON HUT

and unloading. When doing this it is wise to remove your wallet, sunglasses, or anything that might be in your pockets, as objects can easily fall into the hole when you pull your pants down. And believe me, you do not want to try to retrieve anything from that hole. Another potential hazard is the giant cockroaches. They can emerge from the hole while you are at your most vulnerable and find their way into your pants.)

We decided to write off Randal's wallet and move on.

From Djiguibombo we hiked many hours through a landscape that looked remarkably like the slickrock country of southern Utah. As we walked I noticed that **Randal seemed agitated.** Finally he said, "You can't go on like this forever, you know." "I can't?" I said. "No, it's impossible." Then he went on, **"Have you ever had a real job?"**

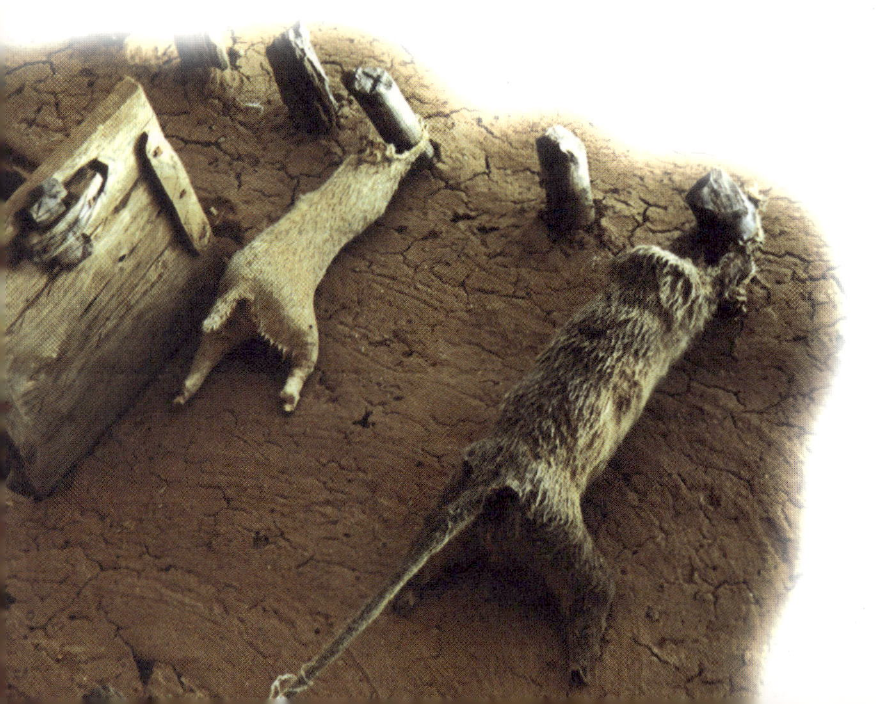

I said no. "Do you know why I **work like a dog?"** "To pay your **alimony** and **child support."** "No," said Randal. "I work like a dog because it's rewarding." "Jesus, Randal, **I work, I just don't have a job."** "Do you have a house?"

"No," I said. "And you've never been married, right?" "Right." "Are you gay?" "No." "Do you think you're happy?" "I think so." Randal shook his head. "I don't. I think you're unhappy, and that's why you **laugh** so much." He waited for a moment and then said, "Do you want me to tell you what I mean by that?"

Luckily we came to the edge of a red cliff, and Randal had to stop talking while we lowered ourselves three hundred meters to the valley floor. Another thirty minutes of hiking and we arrived at the village of Kani-Kambole.

Randal was looking peculiar. His hair was sticking up and his eyes seemed crossed. I thought perhaps he needed nourishment, so we sat down to eat chicken with peanut sauce and drink beer.

(Another warning: If someone offers you something called tô, [pronounced toe], don't eat it. They say it's millet, but it tastes like toe, ground-up old toe stuck together with Elmer's glue. Use it to epoxy your driveway but don't put it in your mouth. Tô is not your friend. You do not need this cultural experience. Just say no to tô.)

THE STRANGE AND WONDROUS MOSQUE OF KANI-KAMBOLE

Baru gave Randal and me grass mats and told us to **sleep on the roof of a man.** We climbed a pole and sat down on the roof of a man. **The man came out of his hut and stared at us.**

Randal gave him his flashlight.

Soon the sun went down and it got colder than a well-digger's ass.

You cannot fathom **the sounds in a Dogon village** at night. **Drumming, singing, spitting, farting, coughing . . .**

40

and the **animals** . . . they seem to be **seeking revenge** for all the injustices they have suffered during the light of day. They **screech and caw and cluck and bellow . . .** and the asses . . . the asses are the worst of all. Dragging their **engorged penises** on the ground, they scream he-haw, he-haw, he-haw, on and

on and on, relentlessly belting out a **bestial choir** designed to torment their oppressors, to make sure that no human being gets even one single moment of peaceful rest.

Then the sun comes up and it stops.

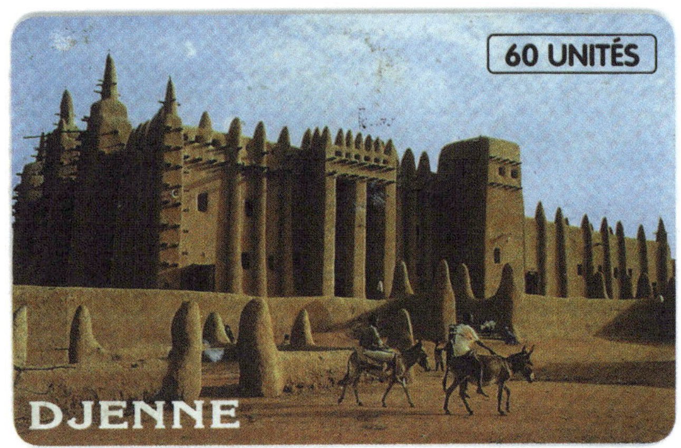

MELTDOWN iN THE LAND OF THE RUNAWAY PYGMiES

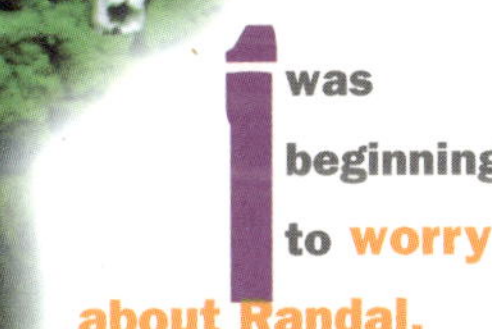

I was beginning to worry about Randal.

He'd already given away his camera, his CD player, two pairs of Levi's, and a Bic pen—and it was only

8 A.M. **What would happen when he ran out of stuff?**

I climbed on the horse cart that Baru had wrangled, but Randal insisted on walking. Off we went, along the base of the escarpment toward the east.

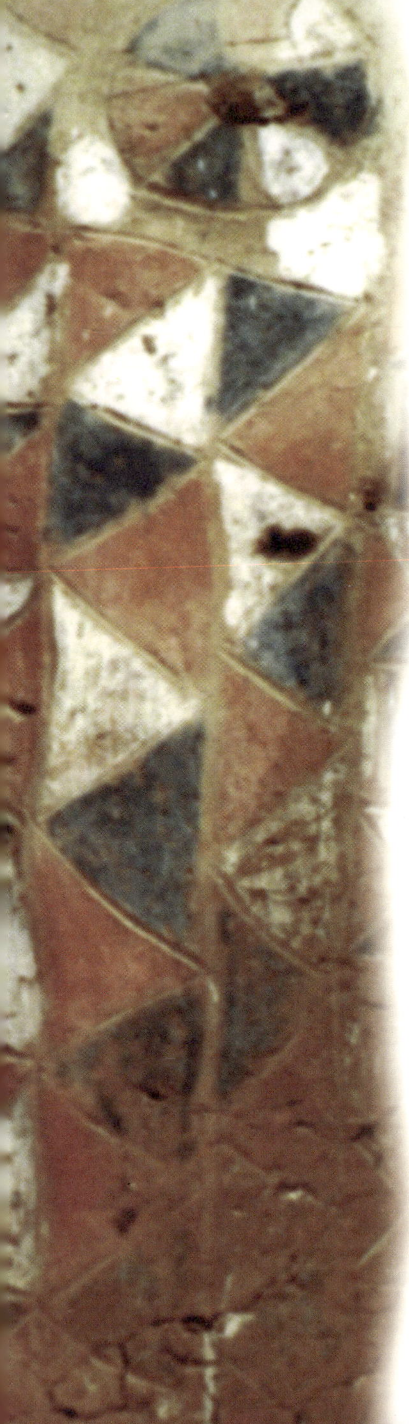

About twenty minutes into the hike, Randal came up alongside the **horse cart.** "Like I was saying," he began, "I don't think you're happy." "For hell's sakes, Randal, I'm just fine." He went on, "And you're hiding your sadness behind your laughter, and you drink too much, and **I'll bet a thousand bucks** you can't stay in a relationship for more than a year." I looked at Randal. He was sweating, and **his eyes were rolling around like marbles in a pan.** "You better put your hat on, Randal." "I can't," he said. "I gave it away." Then he went on. "Have you ever heard of the **Huckleberry Finn syndrome?**" "No," I said. "Well, you've got it." "Good," I said. "You've got it really bad." Then he waited. "Do you want me to tell you what the Huckleberry Finn syndrome is?" "Do and **I'll stick my knife in your throat,**" I said.

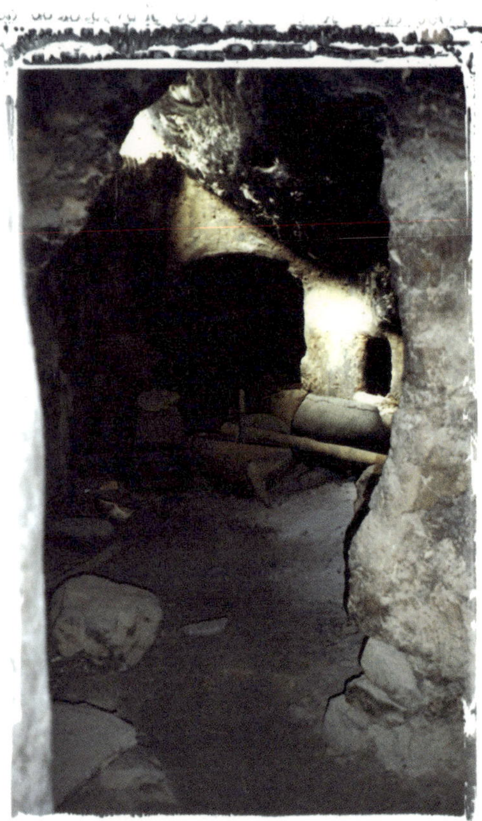

Randal stopped in his tracks. "You're kidding, right?" he said. **I started**

to laugh. I laughed *real* hard.

At that moment Baru walked up. "Pygmy's house," he proclaimed, pointing up at some rubble in the towering red cliffs above. "But they ran away now." I asked Baru where the pygmies had run to. He said he did not know. He did, however, know that they had run away six hundred years ago. I told Baru I wanted to take a peek at the pygmies' houses and we began the long climb up to the ruins.

As one might expect, the pygmies' houses were small and filled with many strange things. There were pots and bones and odd paintings of snakes slithering around objects that looked like pie charts. Baru pointed out where the pygmies stored their millet and where they made their beer. Then he pointed at a panel displaying many tiny fingerprints.

"Calendar," he stated. Embedded in the side of one of the cliff walls were a dozen or more baboon skulls. I asked what they were for and

PYGMY VILLAGE

Baru answered, **"They are for the sacrifice."** "Sacrifice to what?" I asked. "I do not know,"

Baru and I began the long descent down the cliff to the near-by Dogon village of Teli.

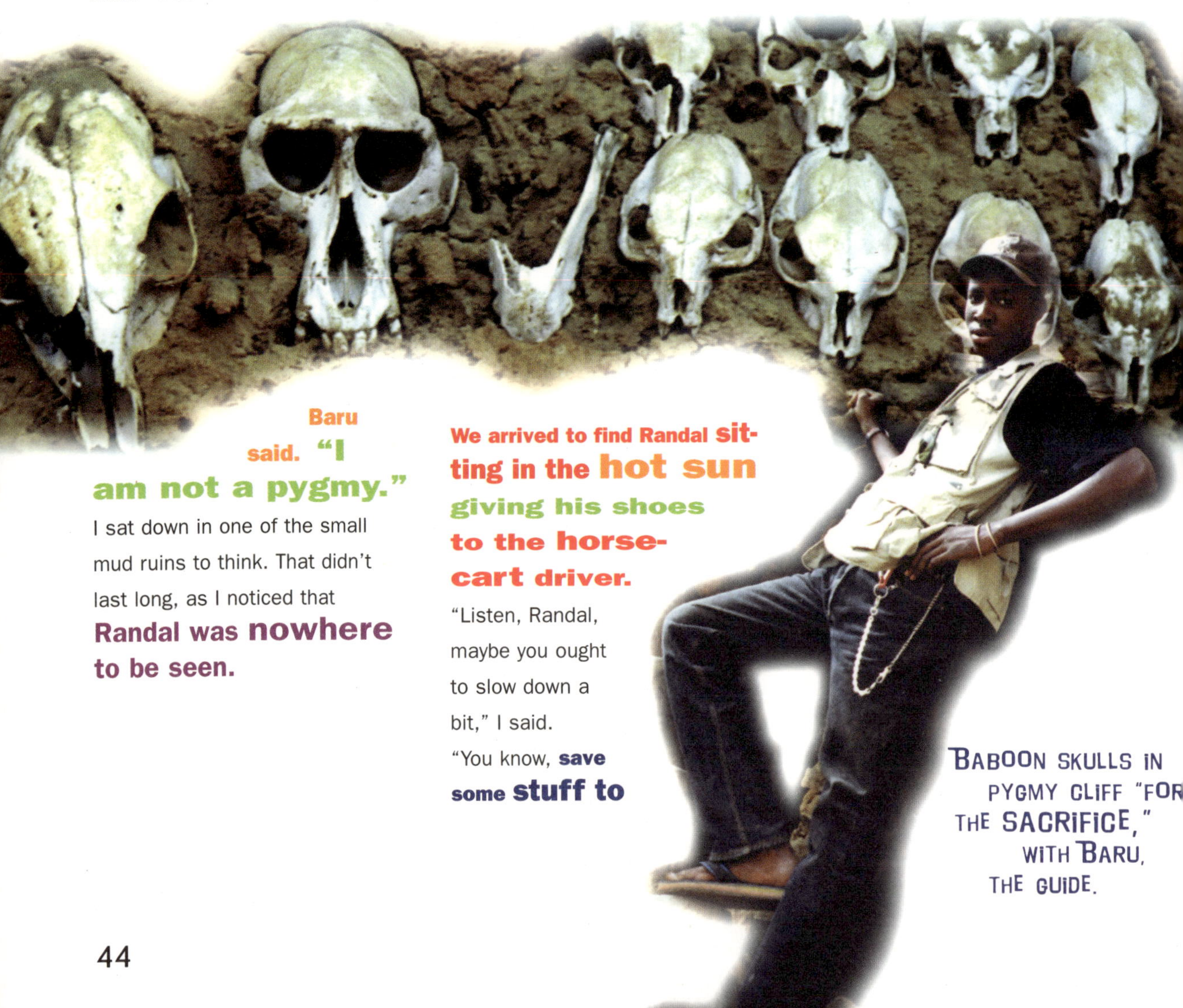

Baru said. "I am not a pygmy."

I sat down in one of the small mud ruins to think. That didn't last long, as I noticed that **Randal was nowhere to be seen.**

We arrived to find Randal sitting in the hot sun giving his shoes to the horse-cart driver.

"Listen, Randal, maybe you ought to slow down a bit," I said. "You know, **save some stuff to**

44

give away later. I mean, you might need your shoes."

Randal pulled off one shoe and looked up at the sky. After a long while he said,

"I know now that **I don't like to travel.**"

"I know now that you are insane."

"I know now that I want to go home."

And with that, Randal stood up and walked away. **"Wrong way,** Randal!" I called out. "Djiguibombo is over there!" **Baru started getting nervous.**

"This is not good," he said. **"People will think I am a bad guide."** Baru picked up Randal's one shoe and ran after him. **After a while they came back. Randal said he was okay now and that we should head on. And so we did.**

Two days later we made it back to Mopti. Randal was looking pretty good, so Baru and I **put him on a bus headed for Bamako.** The driver asked me if Randal had any baggage, and I said, "Not anymore."

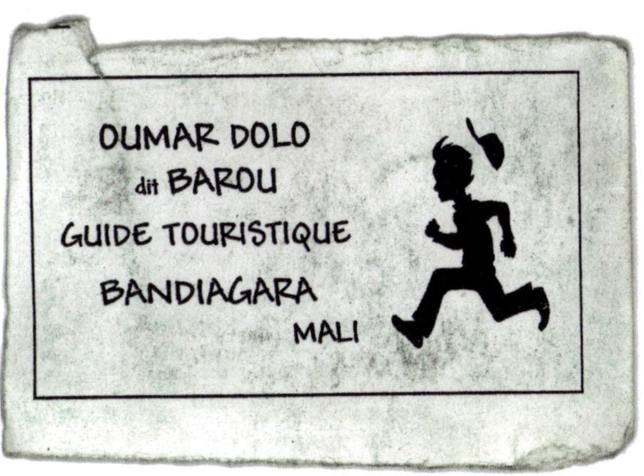

"Okay, Randal," I said as I handed him an envelope. **"This is your plane ticket.** It leaves on Friday. **Promise me you won't give it away."** Randal promised and we shook hands. Baru passed Randal a Coca-Cola and a **banana through the window,** and the bus pulled away. Baru looked at me and said, "Randal is a very generous fellow." I said, "Yes . . . he certainly is."

FLOATING

Taking Randal back to Mopti turned out to be a stroke of good luck. While there I spotted a **big boat** in the bay and discovered that it was, in fact, the last one of the year heading downriver toward Timbuktu. I booked a **first-class** cabin. The cost: about $60 for the three-day trip, and that included three meals a day.

Baru informed me that even though the boat was not scheduled to leave until the next morning, I had better sleep on board that night. He said **the boat would leave when it got ready to go and no one knew exactly when that was.** With that in mind, I purchased six cans of pineapple juice and some **bug spray** from a street vendor, climbed aboard the boat, and went to sleep.

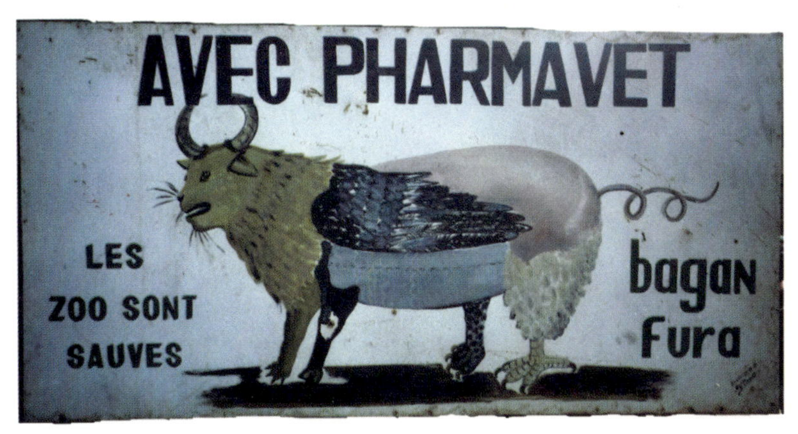

Huckleberry Finn float by on a raft. He looked a lot like Randal, and **his raft was sinking.** I thought to myself, this guy has spent his entire life on the river, and I'm just a virgin—it's absurd that I have to save him. But I threw out a life preserver and felt superior.

That night I had a **strange dream** so I wrote it down. I was in a **blue room floating on an ocean of sand.** Clover knocked on my door and said she had a big surprise for me. I told her I could not open the door because it was my job to keep the sand out and I had no broom. She said okay and left with the **dancing dwarf in a cab.** I was filled with deep regret. Then my regret turned to **embarrassment** because the symbolism in my dream was so transparent. Next I found myself standing on the deck of a boat watching

A note here about dreams: Experts have proven that all women dream about strong plumbers fixing their sinks, and most men have had at least one dream about taking orders from a sassy waitress.

So it's perfectly normal. Don't worry about it.

The boat was already under-way when a **bell rang** and **woke me up.** It was summoning me to the ship's dining room for breakfast. There Mr. Bacha Colibaly introduced himself as the **Chief of Animation.** The chief informed me that it was **his job to play music videos whenever we sat down to eat.** I pulled a chair up to the table and sat down to a plate of bread and a cup of tea with condensed milk and sugar. He started the VCR and we watched **African MTV,** and I'll be damned if the dancing dwarf from the Bamako nightclub didn't pop up on the screen. Apparently he's famous in Mali.

The chief then pointed at a picture of General Abdoulye Soumare that hung in a **broken frame** behind the bar. He explained that everyone in Mali held the general in the **highest regard,** which was why the boat we were on was named after him.

After breakfast I began to explore the *General Soumare.* It had three decks and looked something like an old **Mississippi riverboat without the paddle wheels.** The lower level was crammed with third-class passengers who got their water from the river and slept and cooked right on the deck. The second level contained cabins, **toilets,** and showers for the first-class passengers. The third level was an open deck with a bench and **two lifeboats.** That's where I sat, watching Africa float by.

The **great big muddy river** was immense, and the sky was thick with **smoke and birds.** I drifted past village after village, most with

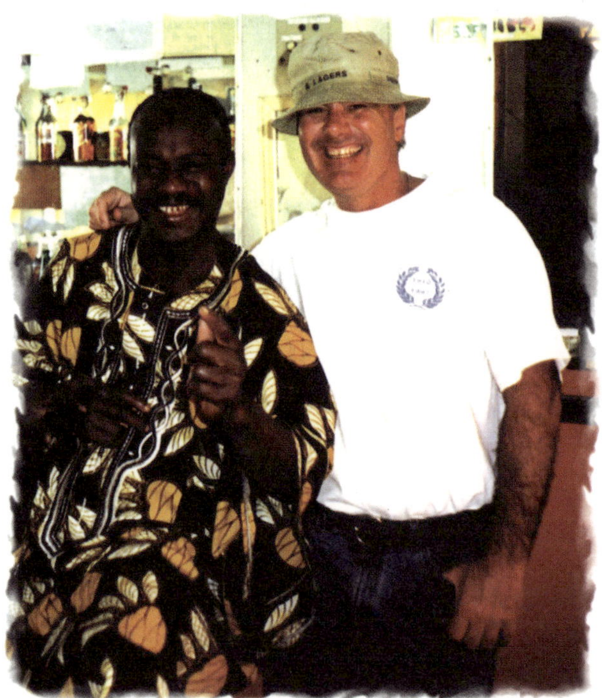

THE CHIEF OF ANIMATION AND THE AUTHOR

48

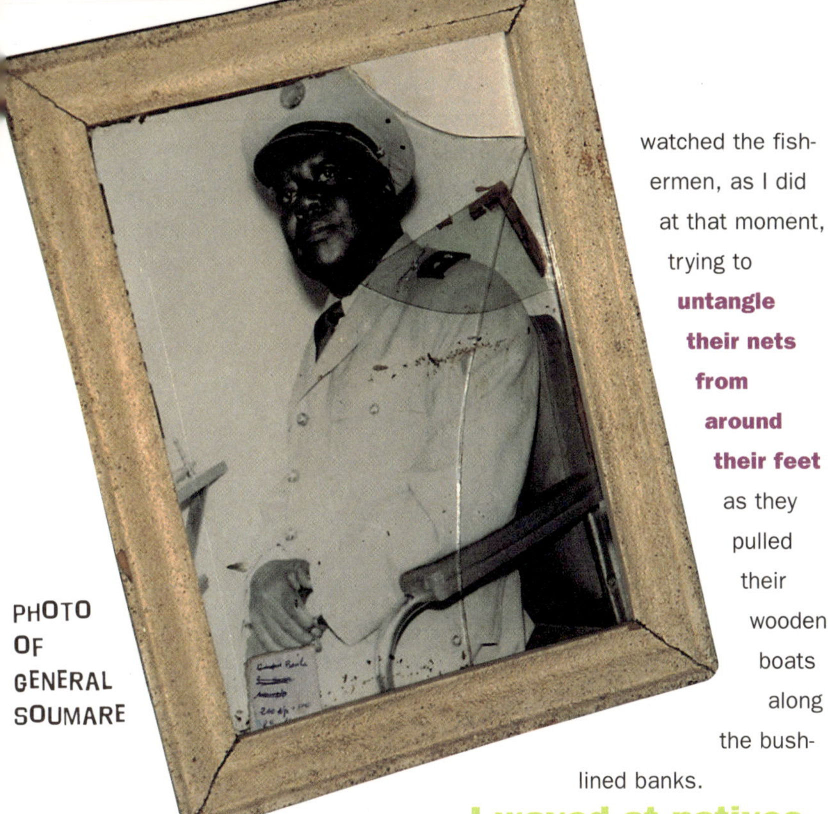

PHOTO OF GENERAL SOUMARE

watched the fish-ermen, as I did at that moment, trying to **untangle their nets from around their feet** as they pulled their wooden boats along the bush-lined banks.

I waved at natives on the shore and **wondered if their ancestors had been the ones to pummel Mungo** with rocks and spears.

The natives waved back.

After a while a student traveling second class approached me. He **offered to send a woman** from third class to my cabin **if I would give him my pen. I told him I needed my pen.** He seemed very disappointed. I shared my pine-apple juice with him, and he asked me if I would allow him to keep the empty can. I said yes.

It was then that I noticed the bullet holes. There were three in the railing of the deck and several more in the hull of the wooden lifeboat nearby. **I asked the student about them. He quickly picked up his juice can and left.** I looked around and realized that I was the only person standing on the deck of the boat. **Suddenly I felt uneasy.** I went below to take a nap.

DAY TWO

A guy can get lonely when traveling so **when I saw the Italian girl emerge from her cabin with a vibrator,**

bizarre-looking mud mosques, rounded and brown and topped with **ostrich eggs.** I thought to myself, this is the same river that the Scottish explorer Mungo Park ventured down. He must have seen these same villages. He must have

BULLET HOLE IN DECK RAILING

I was happy. I had spotted her the day before, drying her thick black curly hair on the deck of the boat, but she had **vanished** before I was able to make contact. Now I eyed her vibrator and immediately recognized the brand, not really a professional model but effective. **She was using it to rub her feet** when she looked over and saw me **grinning like a monkey.** "So," I said, "How do you like your Super Maxi?** Have any problems with the cordless remote?"

She **muttered something in Italian,** and then a slightly older woman appeared from the cabin. She **kissed** the Italian girl on the neck, and they both disappeared back into their cabin.

So . . .

That morning the river became so narrow that the *General Soumare* was literally **bouncing off the banks.** Most of the Niger, it seemed, had seeped out into a **huge bug-infested marsh** that stretched to the horizon on both sides of the boat. Finally we emerged from the marsh into a spectacular body of water known as **Lake Debo,** home of the Bozo fishermen.

The Bozos are a peaceful tribe who sometimes **build their villages** on **enormous** grass mats that float in the lake. I was standing on the deck of the *General Soumare* staring at one of these **floating villages** when the Chief of Animation informed me that **we might see hippos** that afternoon. I asked him about the **bullet holes.** He said they were from **Tuareg guns.** He told me that earlier that week, during the Paris-to-Dakar road race, a band of Tuaregs had opened fire on several of the race's support vehicles. It had happened somewhere near the city of Gao. He told me **we would soon be entering the land of the Tuareg but that there were soldiers on the boat so I shouldn't worry.**

DAY THREE

A stranger boarded the boat that morning before sunrise. He wore a gold ski parka and a black turban. His eyes were nearly as white as his skin, and I suspected that he'd been **eating sand.** I watched him sit down on the deck and take off his turban. His hair looked like it had been cut with a **broken bottle.** He put his turban back on and went into the dining room. I followed.

He ordered a large bottle of beer, looked at the sign behind the bar, and **began to cackle.** I asked him

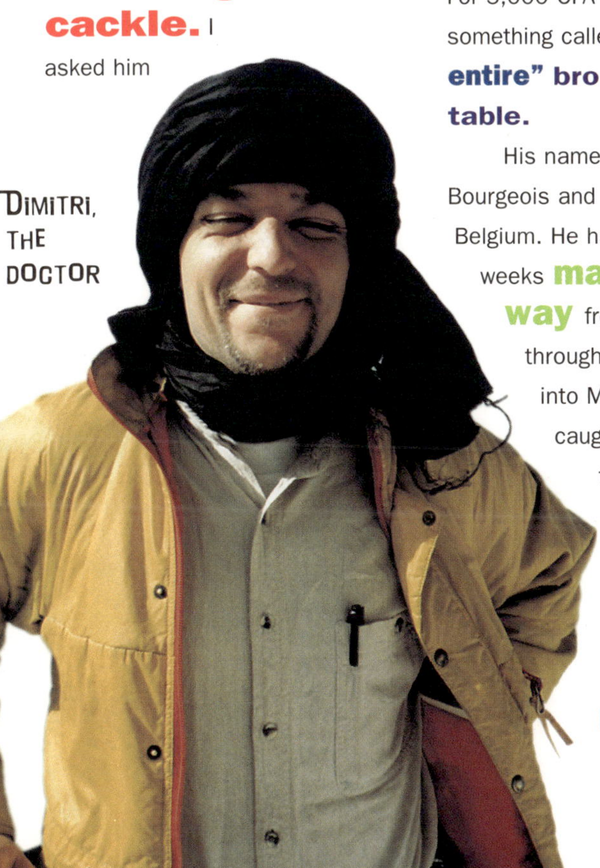

what was so funny. He explained that the sign behind the bar was a menu. five hundred CFA got you a **chicken without feathers,** but for an extra 250 CFA the **feathers were included.** For 5,000 CFA you could have something called **"sheep entire" brought to your table.**

His name was Dimitri Bourgeois and he was from Belgium. He had spent many weeks **making his way** from Morocco through Mauritania and into Mali, where he'd caught the boat in the village of Niafounke.

I told him that I had heard that Mauritania, a land that almost **completely consists of sand,** was one of

the most **inhospitable** countries on the face of the planet. He said that was **ridiculous.** He did say, however, that traveling in Mauritania was difficult. There were no buses or trains, so the only way to get around was to wait for a truck and **bargain with the driver** for a ride. When the ride ended, Dimitri would sleep in the desert and wait

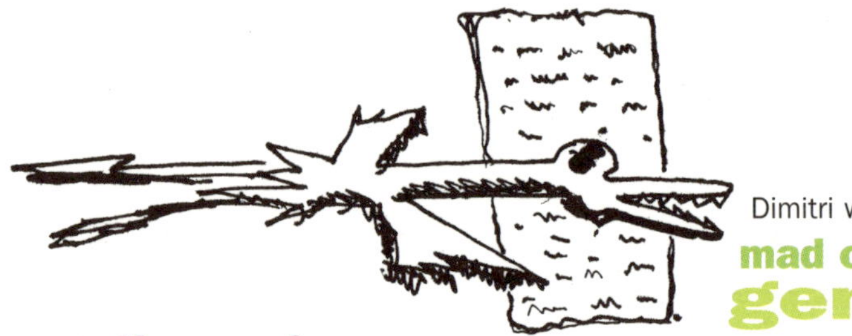

for **the next truck.** He said at one point he had waited four days for a ride that only took him a few kilometers. Then he told me that he drank **river** water. I said that was dangerous and he said of course it was, but if you are thirsty you will drink it. I had no doubt this was true.

Dimitri was a doctor **on his way to Zaire** to set up a small **clinic in the bush.** His backpack was overflowing with medical supplies. **I showed him my thumb, and he pronounced it okay.** Then I told Dimitri that he suffered from the most **severe case** of **"wild goose"** that I had ever encounterd. **He laughed** out loud for at least three minutes. It was difficult to tell if

Dimitri was

mad or a genius.

He smoked too many cigarettes and **drank beer in the morning** and I liked him very much. I hope to visit him someday in Zaire.

That afternoon I sat on the deck watching the Italian girl fight with her lover. Then I noticed that the bushes and trees along the bank had given way to sand and **giant** termite mounds.

A fascinating factoid:

There are

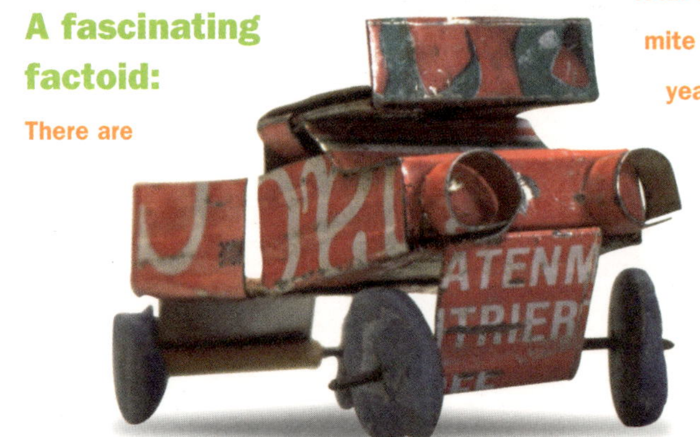

240 quadrillion termites on earth, give or take a quadrillion. Scientists estimate that termite flatulence is responsible for a full one-fifth of the methane gas that is turning our planet into a hothouse. Some say this hothouse effect is directly responsible for the twenty-year Saharan drought that has lowered the level of the river and caused the *General Soumare* to hit bottom, turning a three-day trip into four. Scientists have also calculated that the total weight of termite toots in one year is 76 billion pounds. (Don't ask me how such things are weighed, but I'm sure it can be done.)

About 4 P.M. the sun disappeared completely, and the sky became an **ominous** dark white. **It was dust from the Sahara.** We were **entering the land of the Tuareg.**

DAY FOUR

I spotted my first camels along the bank of the river, and in the distance I could see people dressed in blue. The boat hit bottom several more times that morning, but it continued on, snaking back and forth across the wide river, searching for water deep enough to navigate. Late that afternoon we reached the port of Kabara. I reluctantly **said good-bye** to Dimitri and to the Chief of Animation and got off the boat.

I walked through the crowd on the bank, past a metal wire fence, and into a small open-air market where stands sold tea and barbecued meat. I looked around, expecting to be mobbed by taxi drivers begging to take me the twenty kilometers through the sand to Timbuktu, but there were **no taxis.** In fact, there was no Kabara. The **port had been recently moved** several miles from town due to the fierce drought that had shifted the course of the river. I walked over to the one and only semi-paved road that seemed to be heading inland. Looking around for a ride I spotted the Italian girl standing in the market, **yelling at her lover.** The Italian girl picked up her bag and reboarded the boat. The older woman waited a moment, then picked up her bag and followed. Man, am I glad my **life is simple,** I thought to myself.

Finally, after an hour, I found a **car covered with Madonna bumper stickers.** The driver didn't speak English, but I was able to determine that he was heading for Timbuktu. He **loaded a log** and what I think were large bags of charcoal into the backseat with me. Four other people piled into the front seat with him, **and we left.**

53

16

TIMBUKTU

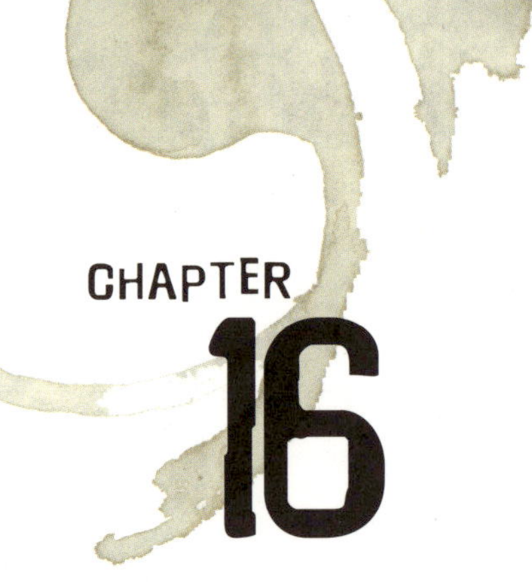

it was dark when I reached Timbuktu. **The driver left me in the sand** in front of the Bouctou, the cheaper of the only two hotels in town. I could see the outline of **dunes in the distance** silhouetted against a sky filled with stars. I picked up my bags and **cautiously** walked into the hotel. There was no one behind the desk

VIEW FROM AUTHOR'S HOTEL WINDOW

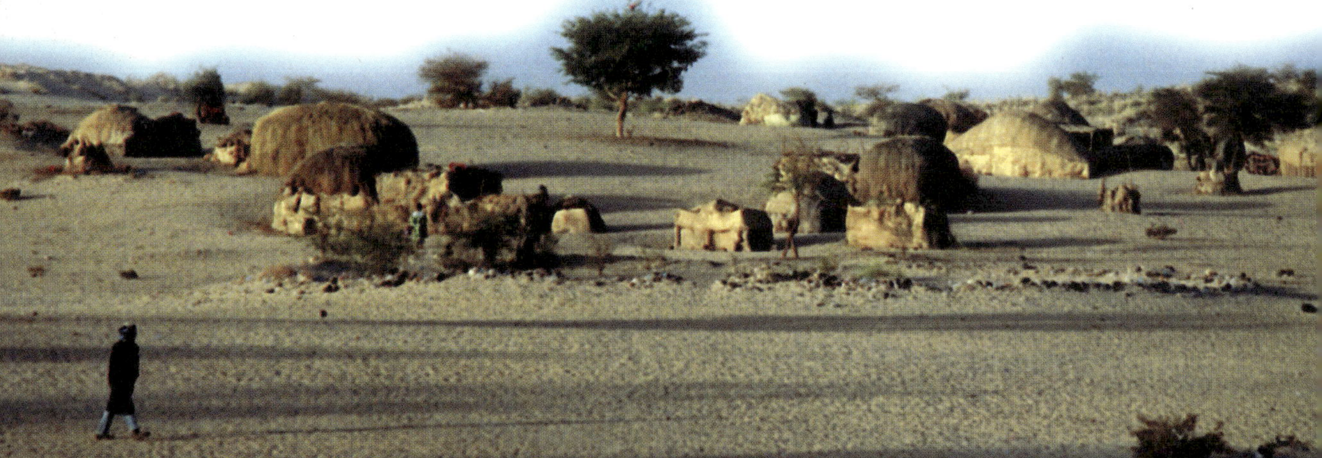

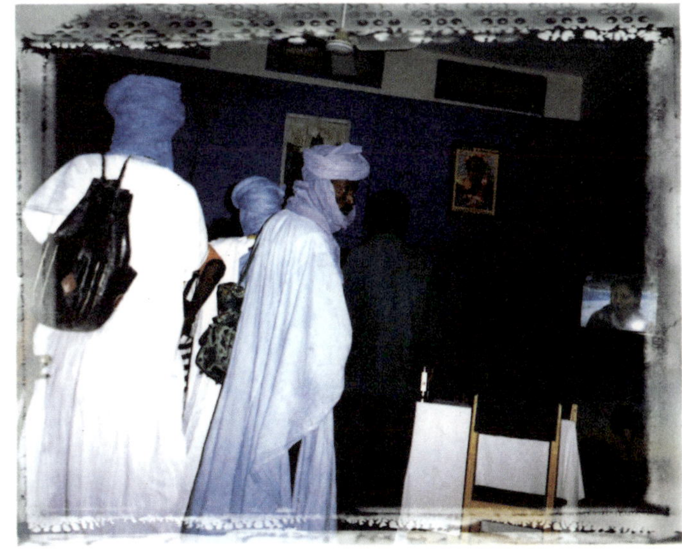

so I went into the bar. **Men in blue turbans and robes lined the deep blue walls, sipping tea** and Coca-Cola. **Tuaregs,** I said to myself. I tried to order a drink using a mixture of Bambara and French. "Castel kelie, grande," I said. **No one moved.** I tried again. "Beer, a big beer, please." Still no one moved. They were all staring at an old television set perched on the bar. I turned and looked and **there was President Clinton** on the TV. "I did not have **improper sexual relations** with that **girl,"** he stated. Apparently **Clinton was having problems with his wild goose, too.**

A Tuareg stood up and approached me. His face was mostly covered by his turban, and **his eyes were hidden** behind sunglasses. He reached into his robe, pulled out an **enormous knife,** and held it up to my face. **I quickly sat**

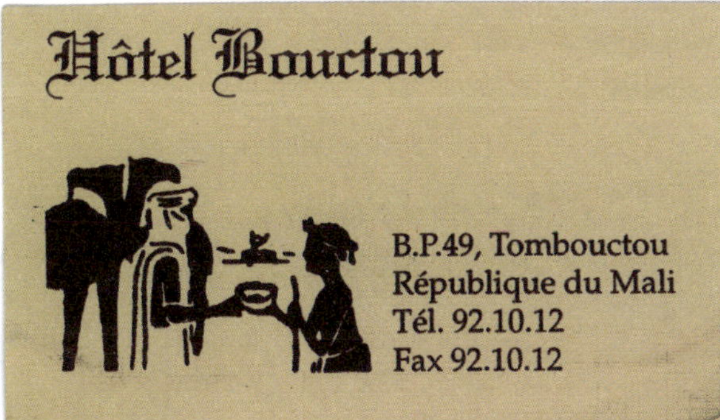

down. He sat down next to me. He drew the knife from its elaborate red-and-blue scabbard, then held the scabbard to his nose and **sniffed.** Then he **shoved the scabbard at my nose.** I had read about the Tuareg and how important their knives were to them, but none of the books had mentioned anything about **scabbard sniffing.** To be safe, I sniffed his scabbard. **"Thank you," I said.** He came back with something in French. I thought for a moment, then took my knife from my belt and held the scabbard for him to sniff. He looked **confused. Other Tuareg men came and sat next to me. They also showed me their knives.** Then a **very large**

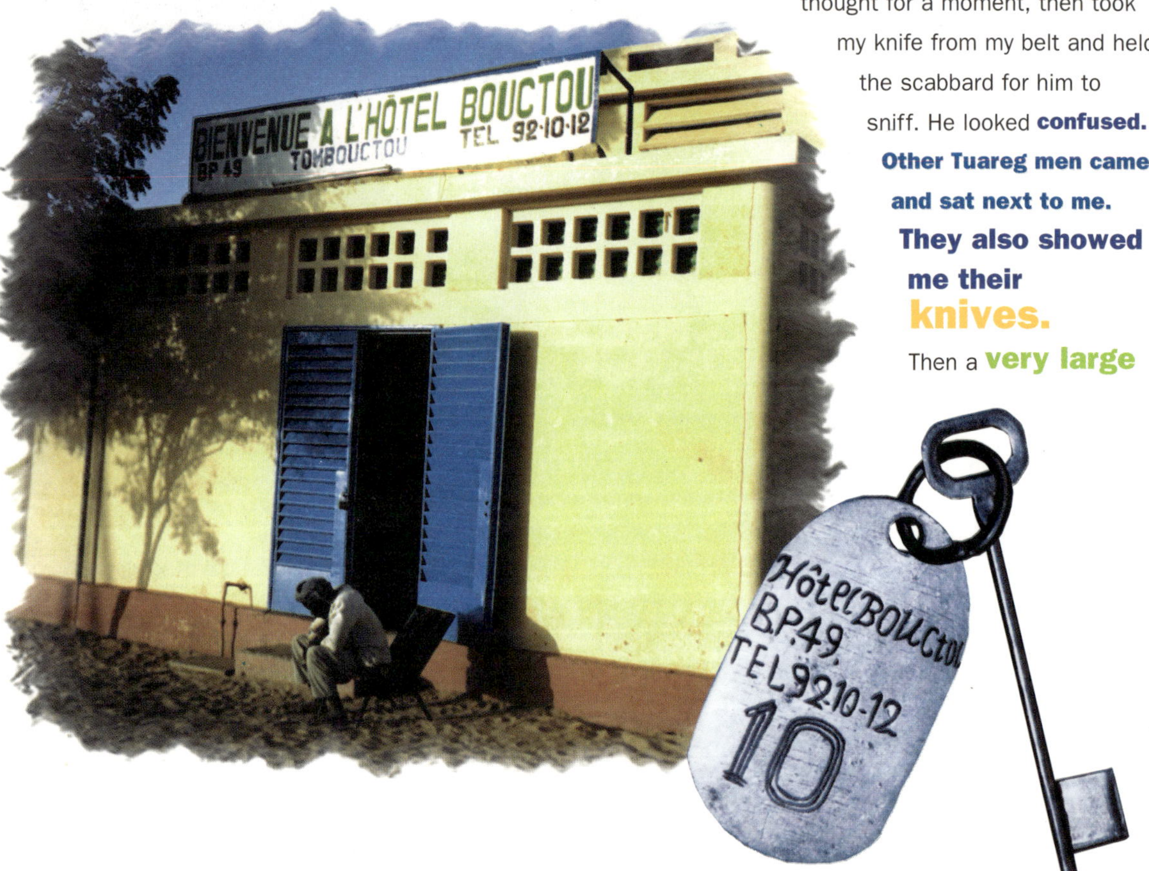

EVEN THE WISHES OF AN ANT REACH HEAVEN.

JAPANESE PROVERB

man emerged from a back room wearing a T-shirt with a cartoon on the front. The **cartoon** was of a **hillbilly trying to mount a frightened pig.** Under the drawing were the words, "Makin' Bacon." "Food?" he said, pointing at his mouth. I nodded. Then I made a motion like I was drinking a beer. He nodded. After some time he returned with a beer and a plate of **goat gristle, grease peas, and salt.** On the side was a large piece of Timbuktu bread. The bread had

sand in it, but it was good. I sat in the **strange blue bar,** ate, and **watched Clinton on TV with the Tuaregs.**

That night, sand scratched at my window and crept into my dreams. I was blue and wore a turban. I rubbed a lamp, but nothing happened. I closed my eyes and rubbed again. Sand began to pour from the spout of the lamp. The grains flowed like water and filled my head, and a genie appeared. "What is your wish, master?" "I wish to see that which is hidden," I replied. "Yes, master." The genie began to sing and dance, and with that, the wind changed and Timbuktu emerged from the dunes, a thousand years older but still the same.

CHAPTER 17

This Place is Just Like Salt Lake City, Strange and Misunderstood

SALT COMES FROM THE NORTH, GOLD FROM THE SOUTH, BUT THE WORD OF GOD AND THE TREASURES OF WISDOM ARE ONLY TO BE FOUND IN TIMBUKTU.

FIFTEENTH-CENTURY MALI PROVERB

I woke up early the next morning, **untangled** my mosquito net from around my neck, **jumped out of bed,** and ran outside to look at Timbuktu. **There it was . . . sand,** camels, mud huts, **and twelve Japanese tourists** huddled in a group around a Land Rover. They all wore **identical T-shirts** with "Blankets for Peace" embossed on the back. They were **nervous** and refused to make eye contact. The tourists were being led by a particularly dashing Japanese fellow wearing a turban and **sporting a big knife** on his belt. He spoke fluent Tamachek. He looked at me with disdain. I looked right back at him with **double disdain.**

I hired a guide

MOHAMMED, THE GUIDE

named Mohammed, and we headed for the center of town. Mohammed was a Tuareg in his mid-twenties. He wore the traditional blue turban, an African shirt, and new **Levi 501s. He'd never been to school, but he spoke at least three languages.** He told me that he was married to his cousin. He said that was common in Timbuktu, and I told him a lot of **folks in Utah** did the same thing. **He then said he would soon take another wife, maybe two.** I said a lot of folks in Utah did the same thing.

Our first stop was the **police sta-tion,** where I was **interro-gated.** The officer asked me where I was from, where I was going, and **what the hell I thought I was doing.** Mohammed translated. I answered, then paid the official **interrogation fee** of 1,000 CFA. The officer put a stamp in my passport and we left. Mohammed then took me to the Grand Mosque, constructed in 1327 by El Saheli, who, I later learned, **invented mud**

ANCIENT LIBRARY BOOK

bricks. I paid the official entry fee of 1,000 CFA and we went inside. Mohammed explained that on any given Friday as many as **three thousand Muslims** would fill the small courtyard and **pray.** We walked through the **labyrinth of dark hallways** lit with shafts of dusty sunlight and came out in another, even smaller, court-yard. In it there were piles of

stones. This was the **ceme-tery** where the most powerful Marabous **(Muslim dervishes with super-natural powers)** were laid to rest. We left the mosque and headed to the library. In the fourteeth century Timbuktu had one of the **largest collection of books in the world.** Some of the old manuscripts were still there. Most were in Arabic, and some were **as big as desktops** and painted with **gold.** Then we went to

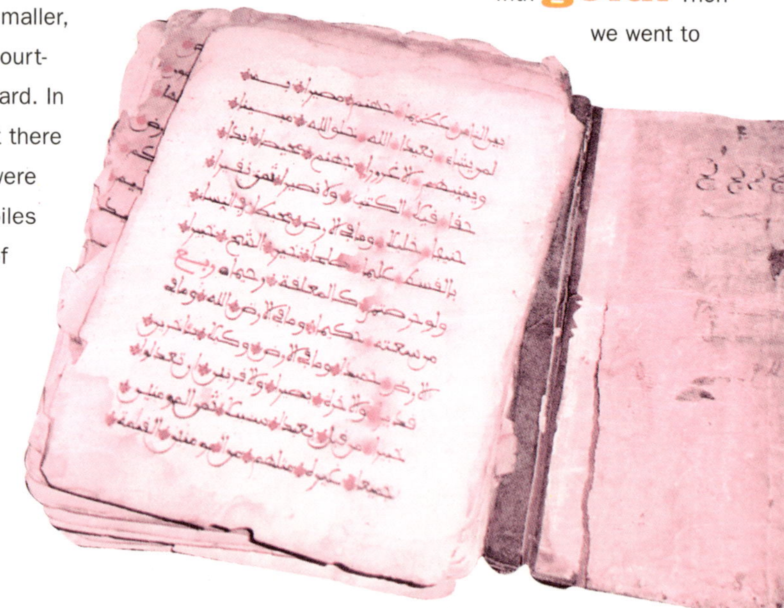

60

the market, and I **bought some incense and a Tuareg tur-ban.** Mohammed showed me how to **wrap** the blue cloth around my head, and **we continued on.**

We walked through the **con-fusion** of nar-row sandy streets mined with **pud-dles of urine** and **donkey dung** until we finally arrived at a house.

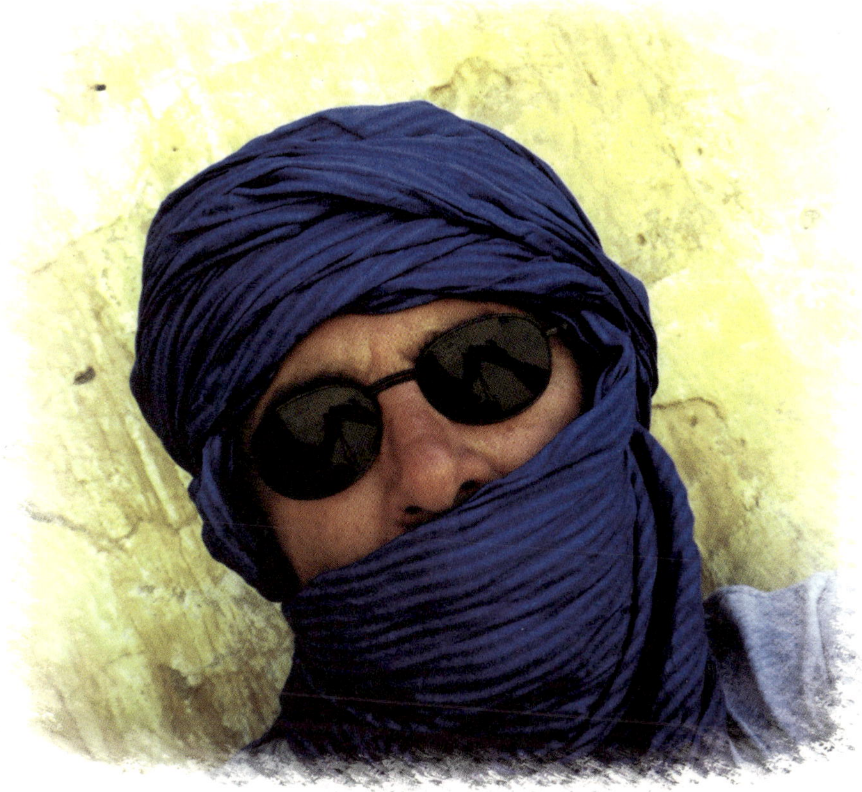

Mohammed pointed at a plaque that hung above a heavy wooden door stud-ded with silver disks. "This is the house of Rene Caillie," he said. **Caillie was the first European to make it to Timbuktu and return alive.**

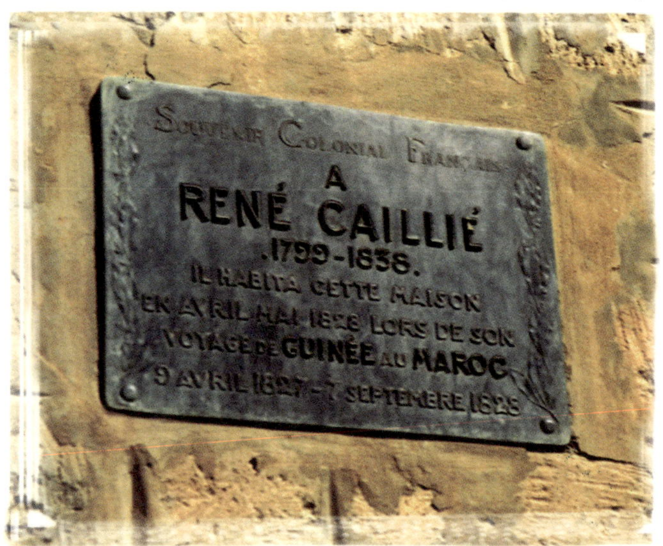

PLAQUE OF RENE CAILLIE

He accomplished this feat **alone** in 1828 by learning Arabic, disguising himself as an Egyptian, and passing himself off as a Muslim. Not far from Caillie's house was that of Gordon Laing, the Scottish explorer I mentioned earlier. I asked Mohammed if he knew why the Tuareg had stabbed Laing so many times. Mohammed said, **"Because he was very hard to kill."** I said, "Yeah, but why did they want to kill him?" He replied with one word: **"Spy."**

Later that afternoon I decided to take a **walk by myself.** Not one hundred yards from my hotel **I came upon a little guy,** maybe ten years old, with a **severe** case of Attention Deficit Disorder. He followed me everywhere I went. He could not shut up. He **drove me nuts. "Here** comes my friend," he would yell. **"He is an American! He has lots of money!"** The little guy was tiny, maybe two foot five, and wore a turban that went way down around his ankles. "Take my picture!" he'd scream. **"I am a Tuareg warrior!"** Pretty soon there were fifteen **little kids shadowing** my every move. If I went to the **toilet,** they waited outside. If I hid in my room, they waited outside. When I did come out, the little guy would yell, **"He is awake!** He is an American! He has lots of money!" Finally I gave the little guy some cash and told him to go to the market and buy me a **bucket of steam.** He yelled, "My friend has given me money! I am going to the market to buy a bucket of steam! **Do not worry!** I will soon return!"

I ran out the back door of the hotel and made for town.

I roamed the puzzle of streets **deeper and deeper into the old part of Timbuktu.** As I walked I began to think about the Antonioni film *The Passenger.* In that film Jack Nicholson is a journalist wandering the Sahara. He meets a man in a hotel **not unlike my hotel,** the Bouctou. The man has a **heart attack** and dies. Jack takes the man's passport and **switches identities.** Then Jack meets the incredibly beautiful Maria Schneider, and together they begin to **drift** from place to place, neither knowing much about the other or where they are going. I was imagining myself as Jack and Clover as Maria when I suddenly realized that **I had no idea where I was or how to get back** to my hotel. The sun was setting and darkness was coming on fast. I picked up my pace and soon found myself at the **edge of town** with nothing but dunes before me. I was about to start back when a small boy dressed in rags appeared from the shadows. He pointed at the street I was heading down and shook his head emphatically. **"No, no,"** he said. I followed the boy as he led me in a different direction, back into the narrow dark streets. He walked ahead, then turned a corner and **vanished.** It was **pitch black** now,

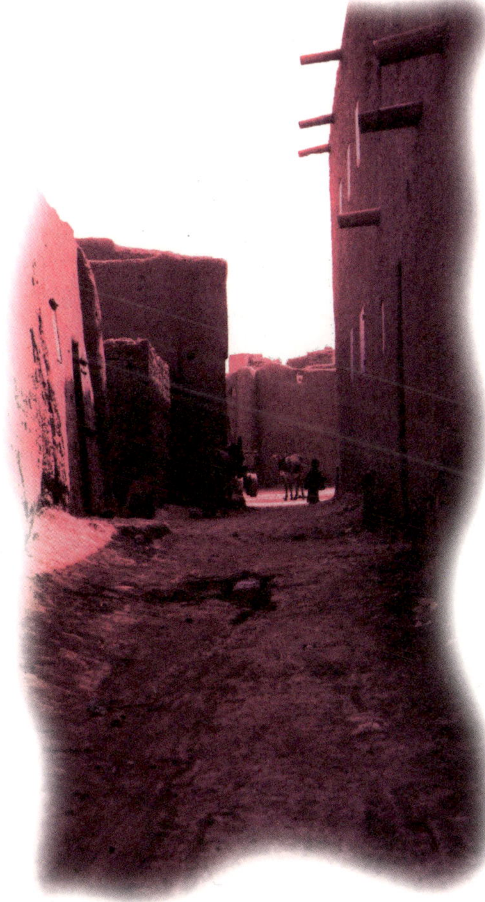

no moon, no streetlights, only the **twisting maze of mud walls** that seemed to lead nowhere. A door opened and **a dark face emerged.** I had no idea what the face was saying, but it didn't sound good so I hurried on. **Two tall silhouettes in turbans** came toward me. I took a quick right down another, even smaller, sandy street. The **silhouettes** **fell in behind me. You fool,** I thought to myself.

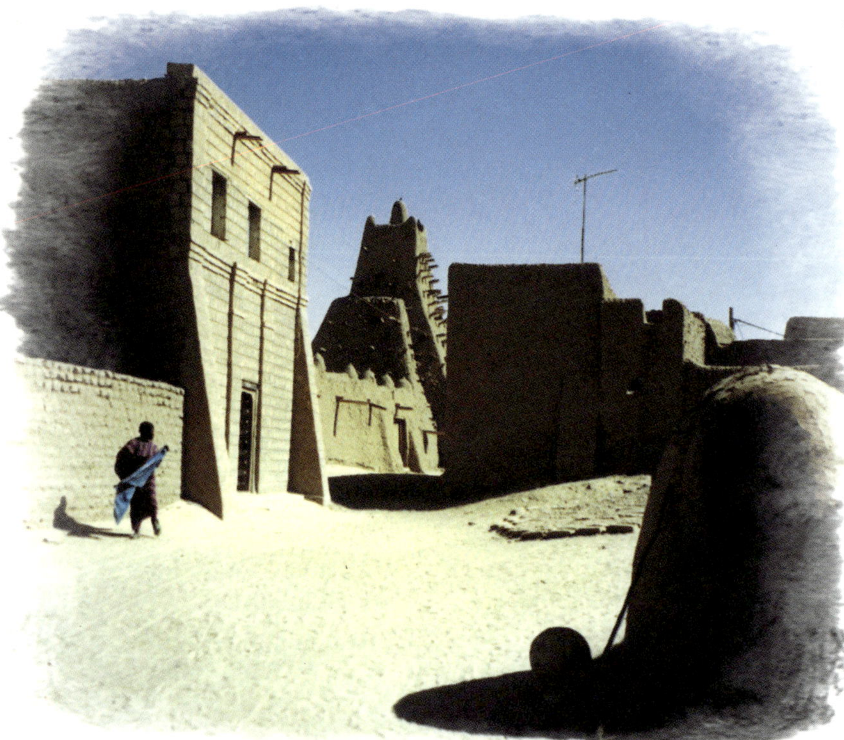

DOWNTOWN TIMBUKTU

Your **pockets are crammed with cash,** and **you're alone** with no flashlight, no knife, and no idea of where you are. **I began to trot,** through one street, then another. Soon I found myself back at the edge of town. I **walked about an hour** out to the **dunes,** far enough that the sounds of **the city disappeared.** I sat down in the sand and looked up at the stars. For the first time **it really sank in. "My God . . ."** **I whispered.** "I am in Timbuktu." **I've never been happier than I was at that moment.**

64

CHAPTER 18

LE ZENITH

Fascinating Factoid: In ancient times, at its zenith, as many as 60,000 camels a year would dump their loads in Timbuktu. The city's markets were stuffed with merchants and traders swapping gold from black Africa for salt from the Sahara. Students and scholars from all over the Arab world would come to study the Koran in the universities of Timbuktu. But now that's all gone. The population has dwindled from 100,000 to maybe 20,000, and dunes lurk on the edge of the town, waiting to cover everything. Various organizations try to fight back the Sahara by planting trees, but that's like fighting a forest fire with a squirt gun.

I stood outside and clapped three times.

(That's what you do instead of knocking.) Amir invited me in. His girlfriend, Fatima, cooked tô and sauce in the courtyard while we listened to **Led Zeppelin's** "Stairway to Heaven" on his **boom box. Amir was a policeman, one of Timbuktu's finest,** and he'd invited me to dinner. He instructed me to sit in his best chair and then he told me about his life.

Amir had spent the day chasing a **convicted goat thief** who had jumped the short fence that surrounds the prison. The thief's sister had come to the jail to collect her brother's belongings. Amir had disguised himself, trailed her, and staked her out, but it was all in vain. According to Amir, the outlaw had **too many evil friends**

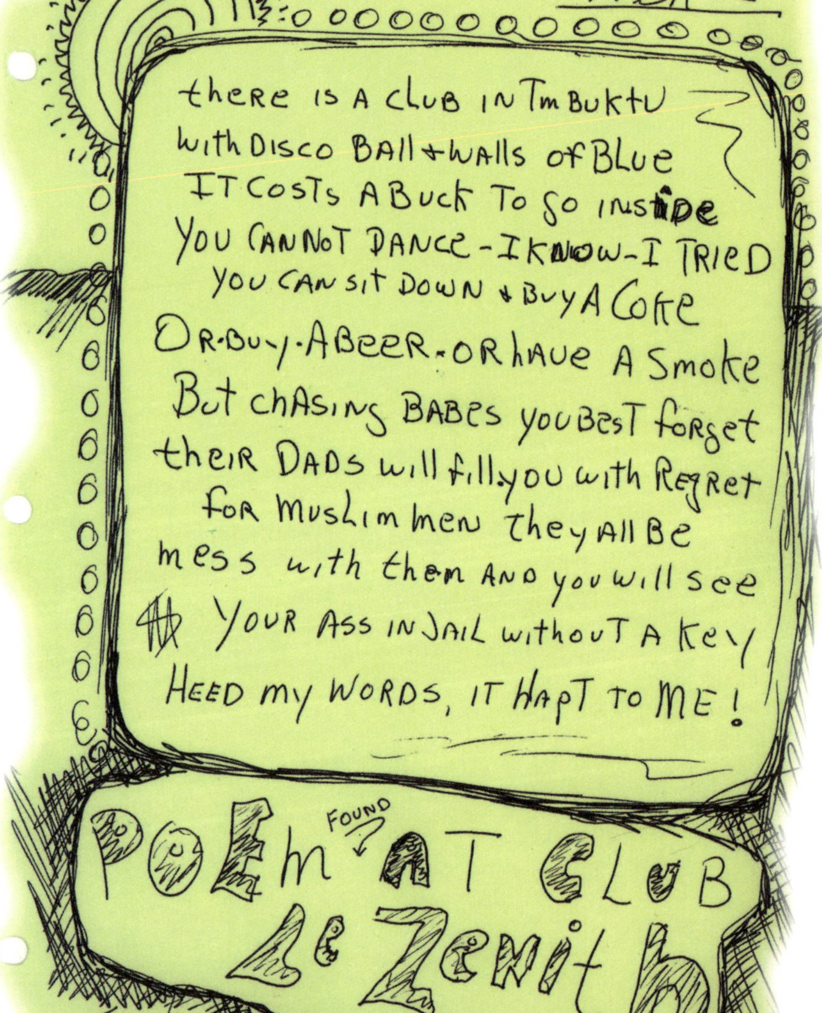

POEM WRITTEN ON A CIGARETTE BOX FOUND AT CLUB LE ZENITH, TIMBUKTU. AUTHOR UNKNOWN

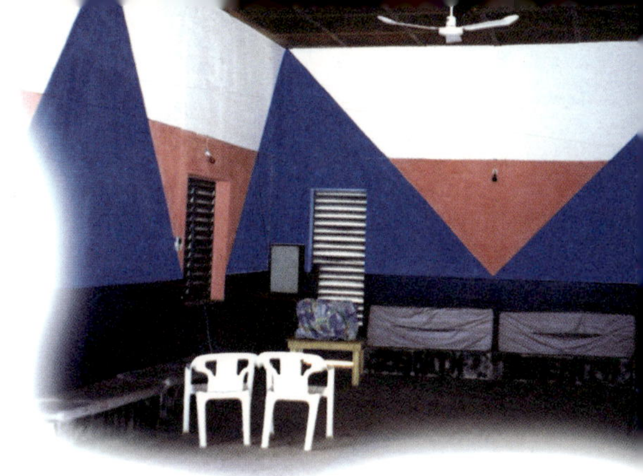

in Timbuktu so he would be impossible to catch.

Amir didn't like Timbuktu. He thought it was **square.** He'd once studied art in Bamako, but he'd been forced to take a job in the army to make money. The army had sent him to Timbuktu to be a policeman. To Amir, Timbuktu was not a mysterious place at all. **To him it was a conservative, uptight, one-horse backwater with nothing to do.** I saw his point. It is one thing to come for a visit. It is quite another to live there.

Fatima brought the food. Amir and I stuck our **hands in the bowl** and ate. She watched, as it is not the custom for women to eat with the men.

After eating, Amir told me of a disco in town. **We decided to go.**

Club Le Zenith had a **one-dollar cover** charge that Amir could not afford. I offered to pay, but he would not accept, so I went in by myself. The club was comprised of **one big room, three plastic chairs, and a guy selling sodas and beer**. I was the only one there so I had no trouble ordering a drink. I asked the bartender, "So what goes on here anyway?" He said, "This is the **hottest club** in Mali." Then he said, "We have no air-conditioning." He went on, "Over there is the **cinema.**" He pointed to a small room off to the side. **"We have no screen and the projector is broken."** Then he said, "I am tired now. I want to go home." **I drank my Fanta and left.**

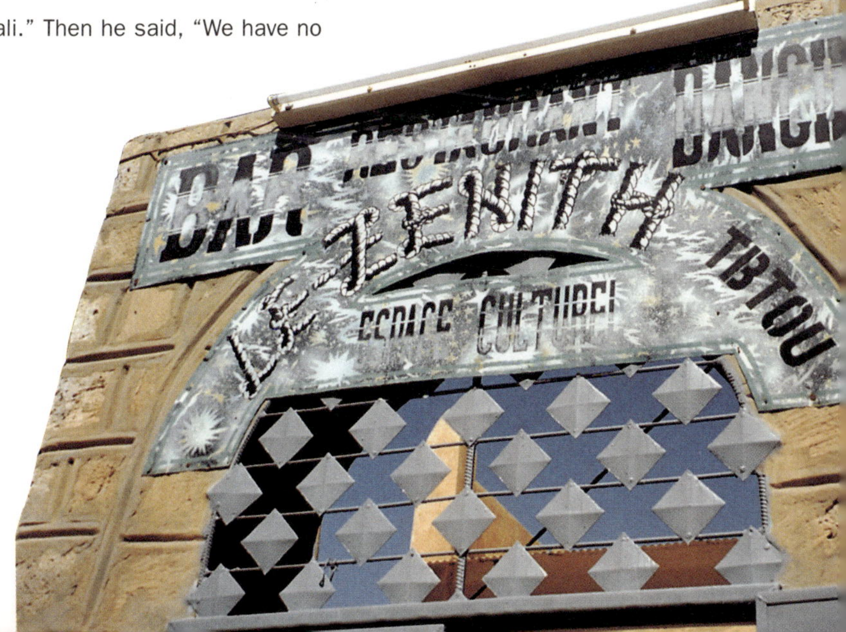

CHAPTER 19

GROUP SEX

Not so long ago I traveled to the ghost town of Iosepa, about seventy miles west of Salt Lake City. I was **poking around the graveyard,** looking at tombstones, when I noticed a very attractive **girl in cut-offs** and T-shirt striding down a hill toward me. As she approached she launched into an explanation of what it was I was standing on. Apparently everyone buried in the Iosepa graveyard was Hawaiian. In 1889 these Hawaiians had been **converted to Mormonism** and had moved to this desolate location in **Skull Valley** where they were to **run a cattle ranch for the Church.**

She introduced herself as a graduate student in archaeology, and we sat down on a bench. She took a drink from her canteen, rubbed her head, and explained that she had been to a **"Fun Party"** the night before and that she had a hangover from consuming too many **Jell-O shooters** made with vodka. I asked her about the party and she explained that a "Fun Party" is like a "Tupperware Party," where women gather at a friend's house, socialize, and buy Tupperware, except that at a "Fun Party" women don't buy kitchenware **. . . they buy sex toys.**

She took a **"Fun Gal" catalog** from her fanny pack and handed it to me. I stared at the catalog while she explained that *Iosepa* (pronounced yo-SEH-puh) is a Hawaiian word that means *Joseph,* and that in 1911 Iosepa had been awarded a state prize for being the best-kept town and **most progressive city in Utah.** I looked up from the "Fun Gal" catalog and inquired as to the difference between a "Squirmy Beaver"

and a **"Wascally Wabbit."** She explained that a "Squirmy Beaver" had **extra feelers** and that a "Wascally Wabbit" had multicolored beads that rotated independently inside a variable-speed seven-inch **rotating shaft** with dual remote controls, making it easy to switch on the bunny's ears. Then she said, "Have you seen the fireplug?" I thought about it for a moment and said, "I'm not sure." She then asked, "Would you like to take a picture of it?" I said, "I think so." She led me to a corner of the graveyard and pointed to a **lonely fire hydrant,** the only remnant of what was once Iosepa.

As I took a picture of the fire hydrant she explained that Iosepa had been abandoned in 1917 and that many of the Hawaiians had cried upon leaving their town, calling out **"aloha"** as they

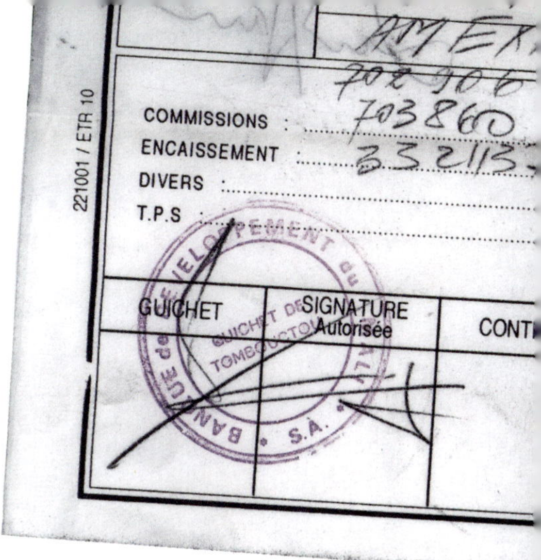

departed. Then she asked me if I knew anyone that might be interested in a "Fun Party." I said I would like to go, but she said that would be **inappropriate** because the parties were **just for gals.** She did, however, offer to show me something in her car. I followed her back, and she produced a **dangerous-looking appliance** called a "Sir Licks-a-lot." She said I could have the "Sir Licks-a-lot" for $69, and that **included batteries.** I wrote her out a check. **She shook my hand, said aloha, and drove away.**

So, what has this got to do with Timbuktu? Nothing, except for the fact that **the Italian girl from the boat and her vibrator finally showed up at my hotel.**

Jena was her name and **Bridget was her companion.** Together we **sat in the strange blue bar** eating goat. I asked them if being lesbians made their lives difficult. Jena said she wasn't a lesbian but liked sleeping with women. Bridget said **she had once been married to a man and that being a lesbian was much easier.**

I told them about the wild goose, and they seemed interested in my theories, particularly the one about **scaring yourself** back to sanity. Jena felt that she was **insane** and that was why she had come to Timbuktu. Bridget felt that she was insane too, and that was why she had followed Jena. They asked me if I was insane and I said yes. Then I asked them what scared them the most. Bridget said, "Nothing can frighten me as long as I have Jena by my side." Jena seemed touched by this, and **they began to snuggle.**

I don't know why but I brought up the subject of group sex and said that I thought it might scare me. They didn't think that was funny and left. **Oh well.**

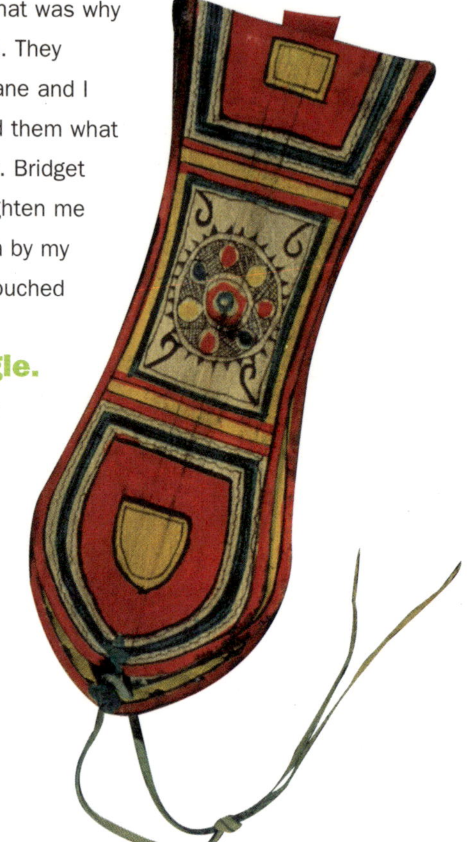

iTCHY AND THE SALT MEN

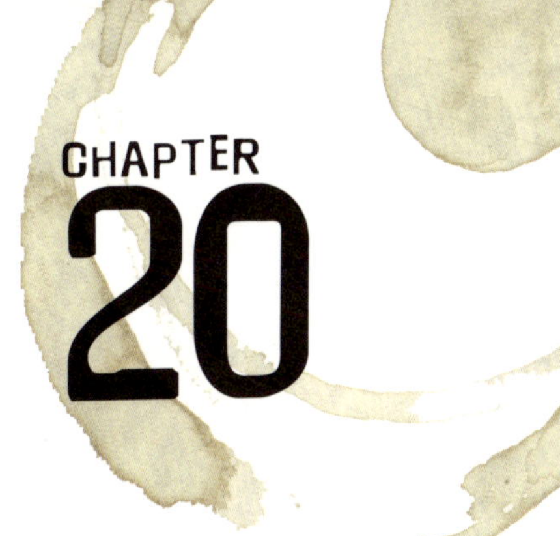

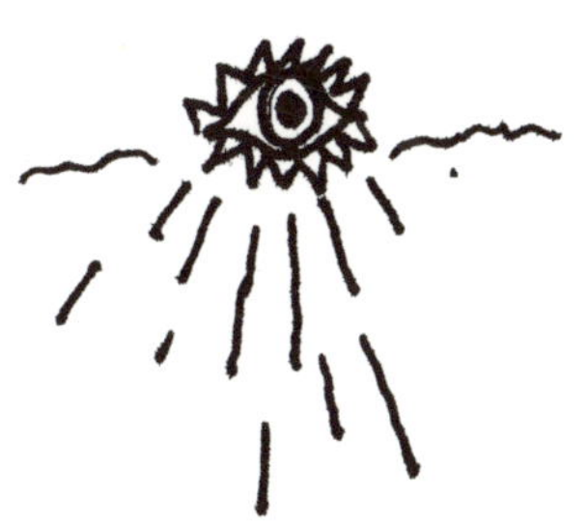

itchy was a **bad machine,** like me and most of the people I like. Being a bad machine simply means you really don't fit in with the crowd you're **destined to hang with,** which in Itchy's case were the eleven other Japanese tourists in his group. He sat by himself, **chain-smoking** Camels, watching the sun go down. I nodded, and he held up a bottle of Passport scotch. We went to the roof of the hotel and started to drink. **Itchy hadn't shaved** in several days, and I don't think he'd taken a bath either. He'd light a cigarette, then **in between coughs**

he would rattle off something in Japanese. I'd follow with a rant in English. Then we'd laugh and **drink more scotch. I didn't speak a word of his language, but I knew what he was saying.** He was telling me that his shitty job back home made him feel like a **fat rat in a cheese farm,** that he detested the worried band of hand-holding, **camera-clicking** country-men he was stuck with, and that he liked getting **smashed out of his pumpkin** with a **fellow wild goose.**

Itchy pointed at the moon and **started to bark.**

Then he took off his "Blankets for Peace" T-shirt and stomped it into the tar.

Then Itchy **fell off the roof.**

I ran down the stairs to the courtyard and found the dashing Japanese fellow in the turban already standing over Itchy, **yelling.** Itchy picked himself up, looked at his leader, and said, "Fuck you, **dork.**" Then Itchy limped back to his room and closed the door.

Anyway . . . once you've seen the grand mosque and watched Itchy fall off the roof, there's not a whole lot more to do in Timbuktu. So the next day, Mohammed and I went out to the dunes to **look for caravans.**

As we walked I asked ques-tions. **"What do the camels carry?" "Salt,"** said Mohammed. He told me that the salt came from Taoudenni, fifteen days to the north, that until recently it had been **mined by political prison-ers,** and that in the olden days the mineral was worth its weight in gold. "How do the caravans find their way across the desert?" **"Stars,"** he said. Then I asked Mohammed why he thought the Tuareg had shot at my boat. He quickly changed the subject. "Old things buried there," Mohammed said, pointing at bro-ken pieces of **pottery strewn across the sand. "Dig."** I dug and asked another question. "Hey, Mohammed, are you a **rebel?"** Mohammed said, "Are you a spy?" I said, "No, no, no, I am a rebel, an American rebel, so your secret is safe with me." Then **I winked. Mohammed got mad and asked me if I was a homosexual.** "No, no, no," I said, "you misunderstand," but before I could finish Mohammed turned and **walked to the top of a dune to pray.**

On his third bow to Mecca he spotted something in the dis-tance. "Camels," he said. "Thirty, forty—there." He pointed. I couldn't see a thing. Then Mohammed showed me how to make my **hands into binoculars** by forming tiny holes with my fingers and peeking. It worked. I too could see the caravan in the distance.

The men were **suspicious** as we approached. I **spotted at least two rifles** and recommended to Mohammed that we find another caravan. But Mohammed said he recognized one of the riders. The rider's name was Diko, and for a price Diko agreed to break off from the rest of the group and take me to his village. I was apprehensive, but

Mohammed insisted. **"It's good for you. Go,"** he said. So **I climbed on a camel named Warren,** told Mohammed good-bye, and off we went.

As we rode across the dunes I recalled what I'd read about the Tuareg, how they'd been fierce **desert pirates** who would raid other caravans, **take what they wanted,** and even **ravish women.** I remembered how, for a

millennium, these warriors had **struck terror into the hearts** of anyone foolhardy enough to try to cross the Sahara. And here I was . . . wearing my very own turban, riding with an honest-to-God Tuareg, sitting on a camel named Warren. **IT WAS EXCITING!**

After an hour we came to Diko's village, a small grouping of tan-colored open-faced tents spread out over several kilometers of sand. We parked our camels

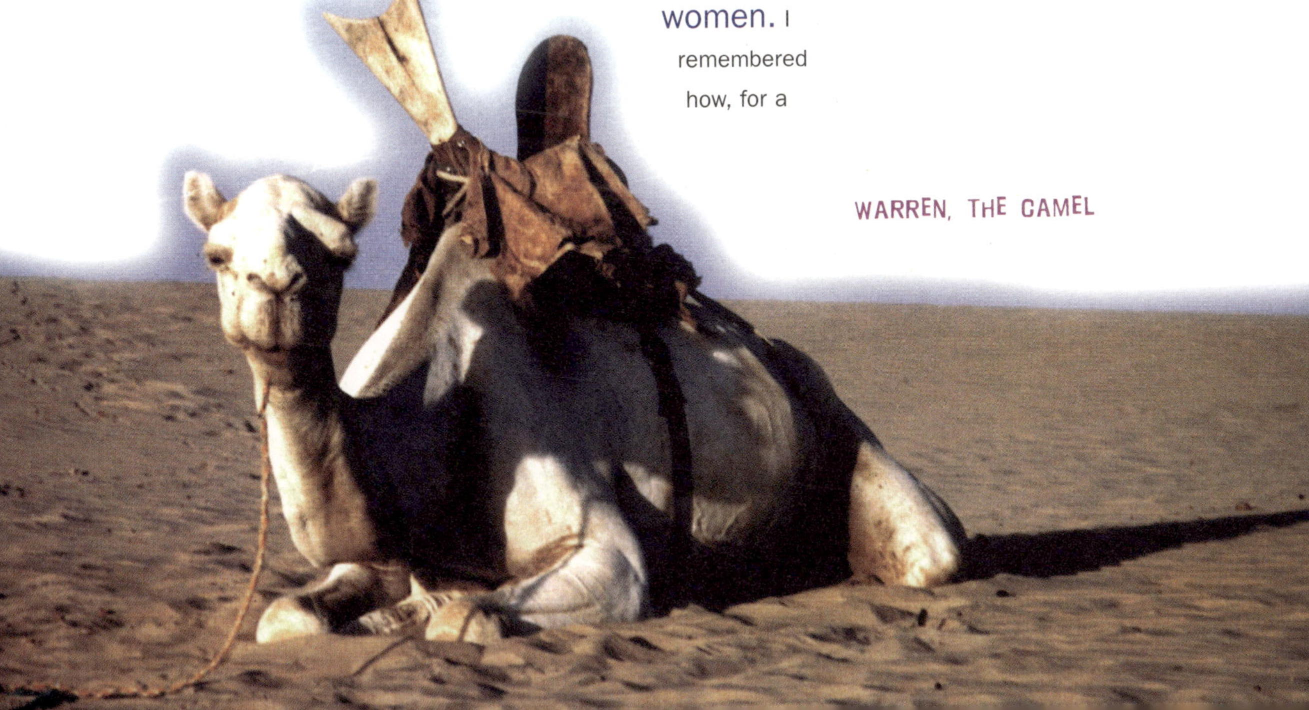

WARREN, THE CAMEL

next to a small well and approached one of the tents. We sat down on **grass mats** in the sand and Diko introduced me to his sister. She wore a deep blue robe and was **very beautiful.** He ordered her to make tea, and she reluctantly did so. Then Diko introduced me to his father, **a small man with a billy-goat beard** who immediately pulled out a **very large knife.** I sniffed his scabbard and said, "Uhmm. Camel skin." "Yes," said Diko. "He wants you to buy it." We finished the tea and went to another tent where Diko introduced me

to his wife, also very **attractive and very blue.** I took her picture. **She slapped Diko. Then Diko slapped her, and they both**

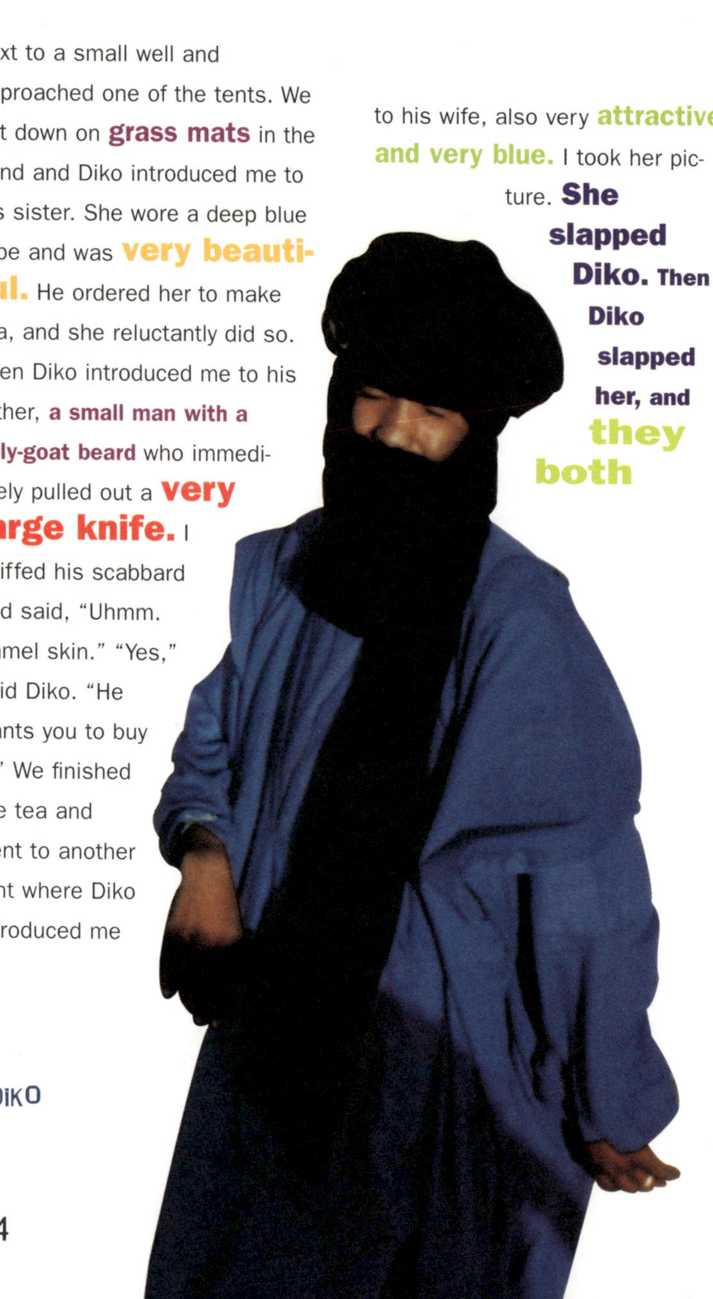

laughed. Diko said he could have all the women in the village dance for me if I had enough money. **I offered him all the cash in my wallet,** but it wasn't enough. **Another of Diko's wives** sat nearby holding a very sick baby. Diko said the infant had **malaria** and asked me for aspirin. I had none. The sun was setting so we climbed on our camels and **began the hump back** to Timbuktu.

As we rode along I asked Diko why he thought the Tuareg had shot at my boat. He thought for a moment and then said, "Because my father does not want to sell his knife."

I shall translate what that means . . .

First, the French really screwed these people big time. In their colonial days they carved up Africa and created countries, **paying no attention** whatsoever to the traditional empires that had existed for centuries.

So for many years the Tuareg, who are heart-and-soul desert nomads, were governed by suits in Bamako who know little of life in the Sahara. **Guess who gets the short end of any stick** the government happens to come up with? This, plus a **twenty-year drought** that would break anyone's balls, has left them **penniless.**

Of course the noble Blue People don't want to sell their

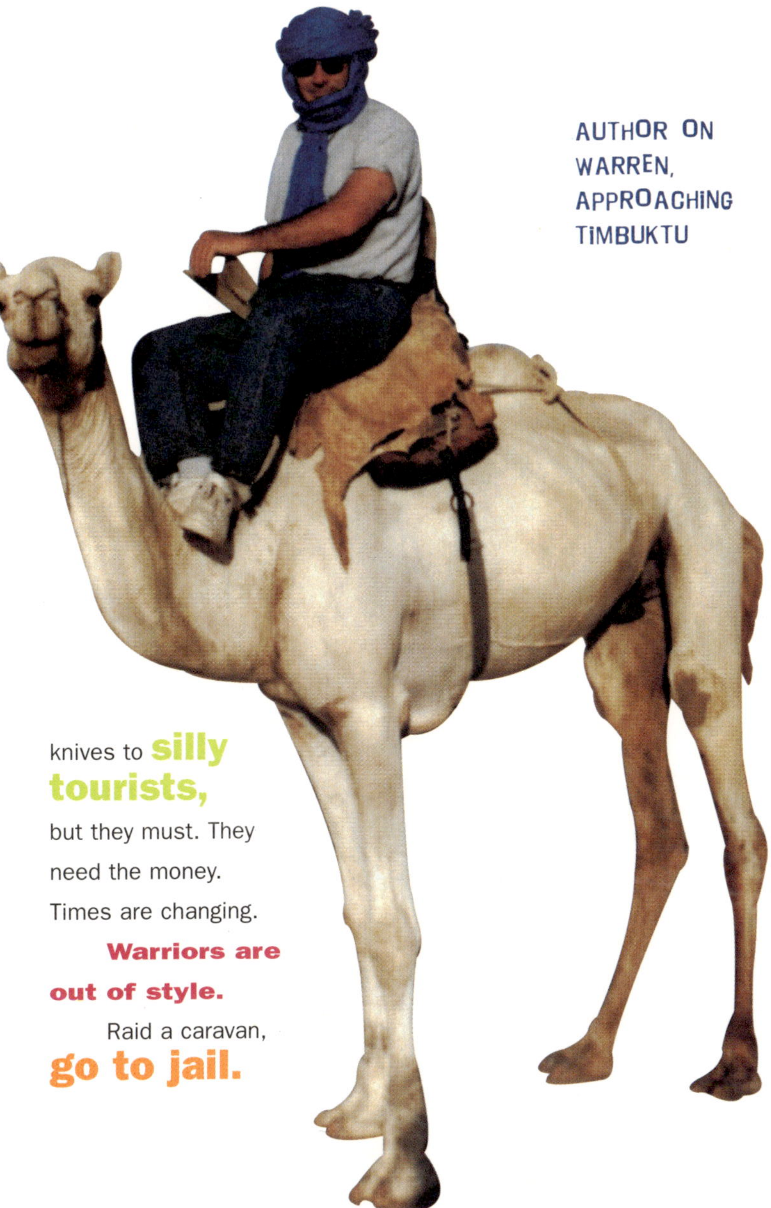

knives to **silly tourists,** but they must. They need the money. Times are changing. **Warriors are out of style.**

Raid a caravan, **go to jail.**

AiR MAYBE

DESiRES ARE NOURiSHED BY DELAYS.

ENGLISH PROVERB

Just before I'd set out on my trip to Africa my friend Scott had pulled me aside. He said, "Whatever you do, Trent, make sure to **go to the well** in Timbuktu." He said that if I did this and sat there long enough, many things would become clear to me. He said this would happen because the wild goose had taken me on a long and arduous journey, a kind of **inner voyage of discovery,** and that journey would end at the well, which was symbolic because, you know . . . **water, life, woman with a big belly button, navel of the earth . . .** birth, rebirth, afterbirth . . . all that stuff. Well, I sat there and it wasn't happening. All I could think about was Clover's belly button. I wondered if she'd had it pierced. I also wondered if she was still waiting for me in Bamako.

Leaving Timbuktu was turning out to be more difficult than getting there. The flight on **Air Mali (known** to the experienced traveler **as Air Maybe)** that was supposed to leave on Monday didn't. The one on Wednesday wasn't going where I wanted to go. I booked a flight on Thursday, but it didn't come either. I tried to call Clover in Bamako and tell her I was stranded, but **she didn't have a phone, and the only one I could find in Timbuktu didn't work worth a shit.** After several tries I was finally able to leave a message at the Peace Corps house in Bamako that I would call at 9 A.M. the next day. Clover got the message, and at last I was able to speak with her. I told her I was **stuck in Timbuktu.** She said not to worry. She would

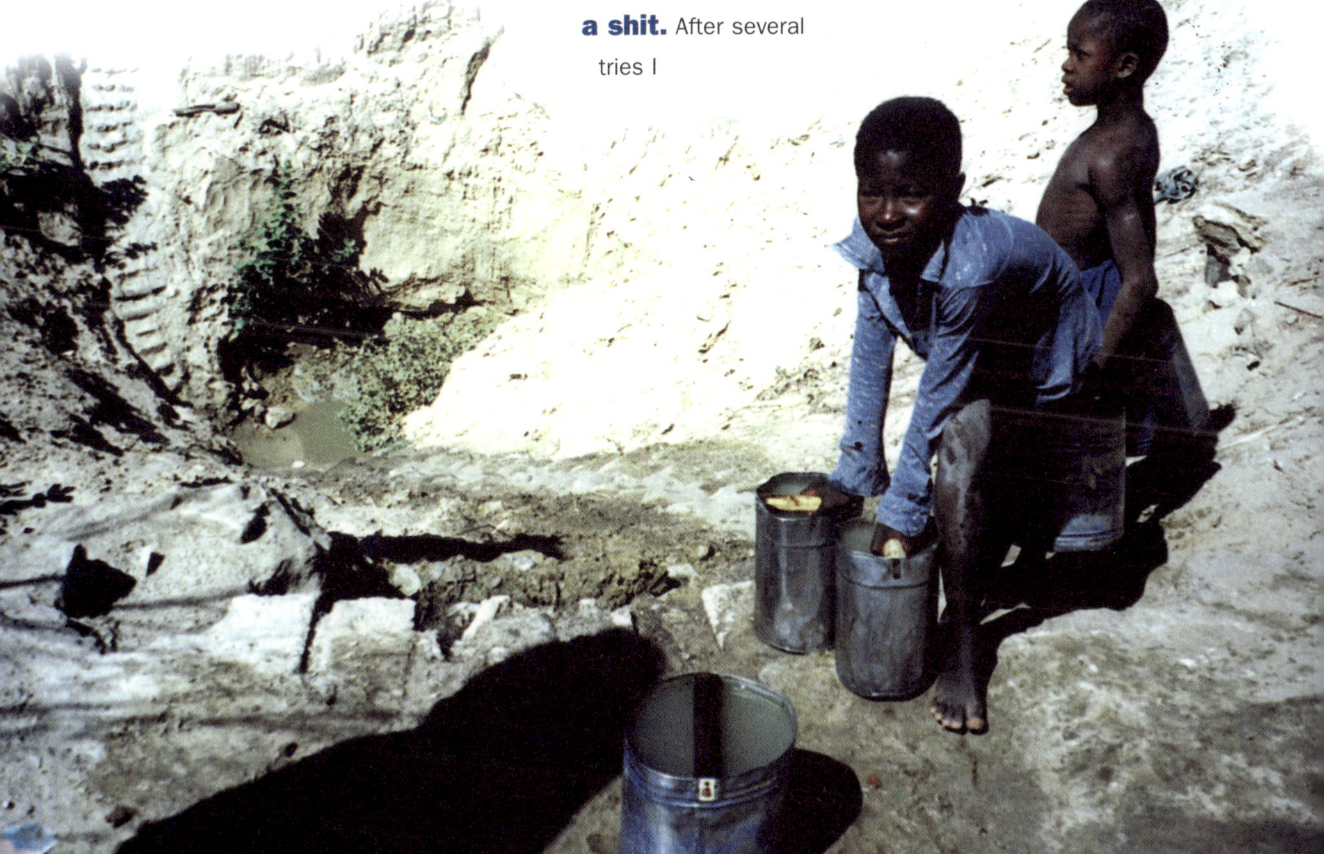

see me **when I got** to Bamako.

Finally I was able to book a ticket, hire a car, and head for the airport. A few miles from the terminal we came upon a roadblock. **Some old fart had dragged a log across the road and was demanding the official 1,000 CFA airport entry fee** before he'd move it. My driver was not about to fork it over. **They argued.** They bickered. I feared I would miss another flight. "Son of a bitch!"

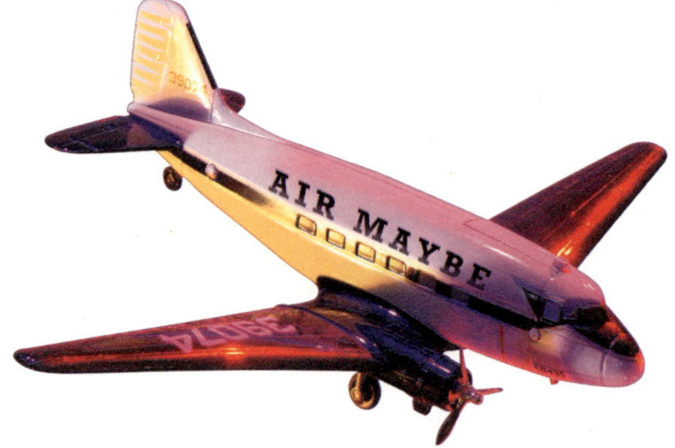

I screamed. **"I'll pay the money!"** and I handed my driver the cash. He stuck it in his pocket, **stepped on the gas,** took a hard right, and drove into a thicket of bushes. We emerged from the bushes, dropped into a gully, and **got stuck in the sand.** I jumped out and started to push. I looked back. **The old fart was running toward me with a big stick.** The car lurched forward. I ran and had to jump in or the driver would have

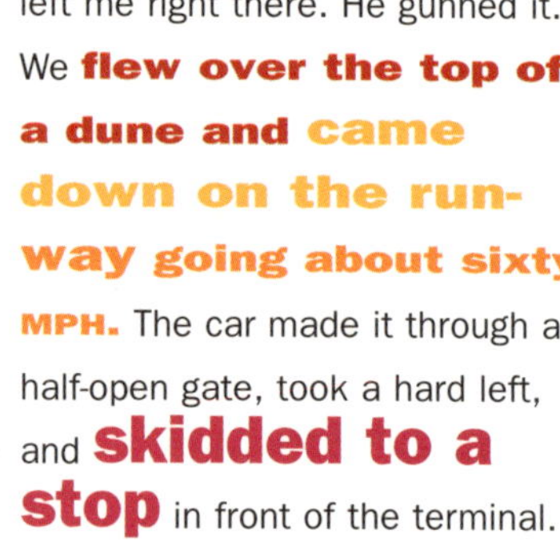

left me right there. He gunned it. We **flew over the top of a dune and came down on the runway going about sixty MPH.** The car made it through a half-open gate, took a hard left, and **skidded to a stop** in front of the terminal.

The plane was two hours late, and when it did arrive it was already filled with people. I managed to get a seat, but two Dutch tourists were not as lucky. **Somehow they convinced the pilots, who were Russian, to let them cram into the cockpit.** The **propellers** began to **whirl,** the wings began to shake, the flight attendant fell down in the middle of the aisle, and **off we went.**

HOSTEL OF THE GREEN CHICKEN

Once I was sitting at home, minding my own business, when Warren Beatty called me up and asked me if I wanted to go to dinner . . . so I did. The movie deal he was proposing turned out to be a complete sham. He knew that I was friends with Sean Penn and he knew who Penn was married to. I think I was just a pawn in some perverted scheme Beatty cooked up to get into Madonna's pants. Well, that's what he wanted, and that's what he got, and all I can say is, it serves him right. Madonna is enough to scare the shit out of anybody. Beatty and Madonna eventually broke up (big surprise), but that's not my point. My point is:

Be careful what you want because you just might get it.

Which brings me to another point.

I started off on my journey to Africa **looking for danger.**

Well, I was **just about** to find it.

Clover and I hooked up early the next morning in Bamako. We bought some food, then **squeezed onto a bus** and began the six-hour ride to the town of Koutiala. The plan was to spend a few days there so Clover could take care of some business, then head for her village, Nankorola.

We rode. We jabbered. We napped. We jabbered some more. Clover told me that a few days after I left for Timbuktu **our Moroccan friend had made a pass at her over coffee.** She had let him know, in no uncertain terms, that she already had a boyfriend, and that was the end of Mr. Morocco. I gave Clover a **stick of gum,** and she went on. Her boyfriend, whom she'd met in Mali, had spent a year in the bush researching **chimpanzees.** It must have been a difficult job because in that entire time he'd never spotted one single chimp. He did, however, pick up a lot of their **scat,** which he used to find out whatever it is you find out by closely examining such things. I was curious about what kind of man spends **a year studying chimp turds.** She said he was a very interesting fellow and that they got along tremendously. Then **she popped** her gum and said, "He's gone back to the States." Then she asked me if I was going back to Mopti after visiting her village, and I said yes. **"Good,"** she said. "I will go with you."

We arrived in Koutiala, an African version of a truck-stop town where big rigs

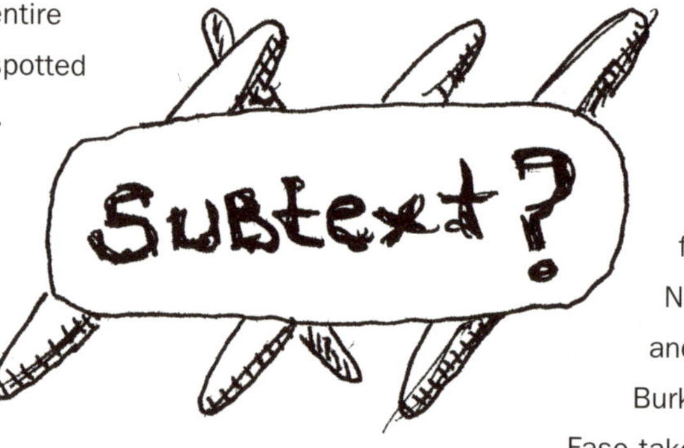

from Niger and Burkina Faso take on gas while their drivers look for **prostitutes** and food.

Clover and I went to something called a Peace Corps stage, which is basically a walled compound where folks in the Peace Corps spend weekends, do their laundry, and gossip before returning to their respective villages. Clover informed me that **we would be roommates,** and we stashed our bags.

That night Clover made good on her promise to show me what Africa was really like. First she said, **"Hey, Trent, what say we go to a brothel?"** I said, "Good idea, Clover!" . . . so we did. The brothel was called **Hostel of the Green Chicken,** and after eating the chicken in the restaurant, it was

Clover went right to work. She was involved in what seemed to me to be a **futile attempt to save a** **vanishing** **language** called Miniakan. She helped orchestrate efforts to come up with an alphabet and record stories. There were also hopes to create some kind of cultural center. For her labor she received about $150 a month and a **mud shack** to sleep in.

clear how the place got its name.

Clover noticed one of the **prostitutes** sitting at a table nearby. She said she thought the woman was particularly attractive. I said, "Clover, **that attractive woman is a man."** Clover was skeptical until I pointed out that the prostitute needed a shave. Then Clover informed me that the reason we had come to the Green Chicken was to say good-bye to one of the prostitutes she had befriended.

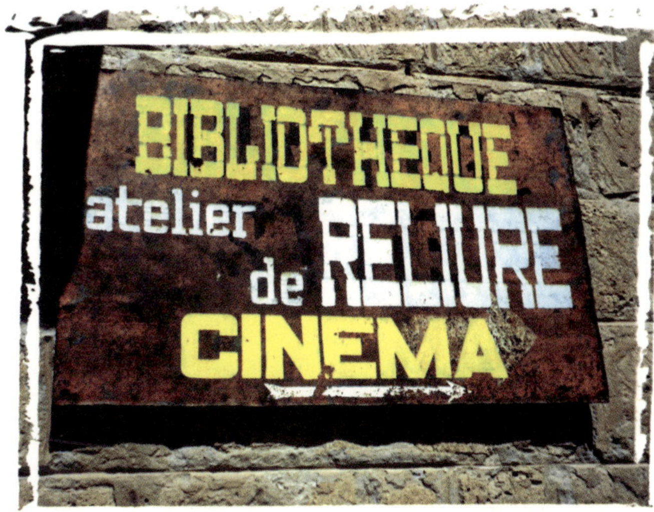

The girl was sad to hear that Clover would soon be leaving Africa and asked Clover to give her something as **a** **remembrance.** **Clover pulled the elastic** **band from her hair** and handed it to the girl. Clover asked for something in return but the prostitute had nothing to give.

The night was still young so we went to an African movie, which was actually an American movie dubbed in French. **Tickets were twenty cents more if we wanted to sit together.** I paid the extra, and we entered the empty theater. **The screen was a mud wall painted white.** There was no roof so we sat under the stars on a metal bench. As I watched the film, which starred Julie Delphi and Eric Stoltz, I thought to myself, **shit, this movie makes even less sense than the ones I make.** Then I realized that the projectionist had the reels out of order, which actually made the movie a lot more interesting, and that reminded me . . .

When I was a kid in Idaho, I'd drive my pickup to the Pud Drive-In on Friday nights. It was actually the Spud Drive-In, but the S fell off the sign and everybody liked it better that way. Anyway, the reels were always out of order there, too. In fact, I was probably twenty years old before I saw a movie with the reels in the right order. My old professor at the American Film Institute said he thought this might account for my filmmaking style, which he called Idahodian Infantilism.

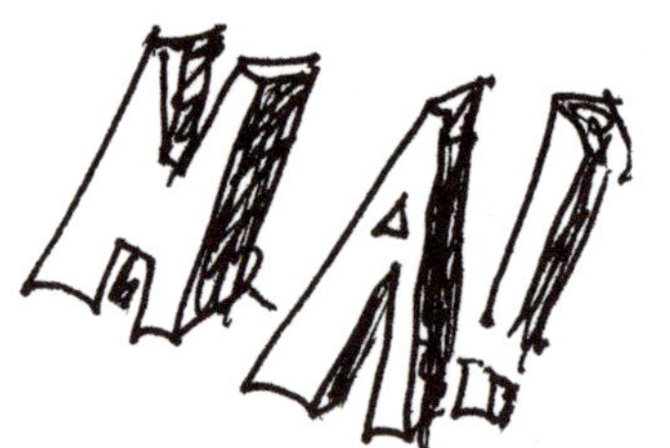

Anyway, I've always liked Julie Delphi and always thought **Eric Stoltz was a putz,** so watching him on top of her in bed was positively **excruciating.** It just seemed wrong. It was like **mixing mud with caviar.**

We walked back to the Peace Corps stage.

I took off my clothes, climbed into my bunk, and pulled my sheet up over my head.

I listened carefully as Clover slipped into her bed.

So, you're thinking, where's the danger? Well, it's creeping up in increments, so just be patient.

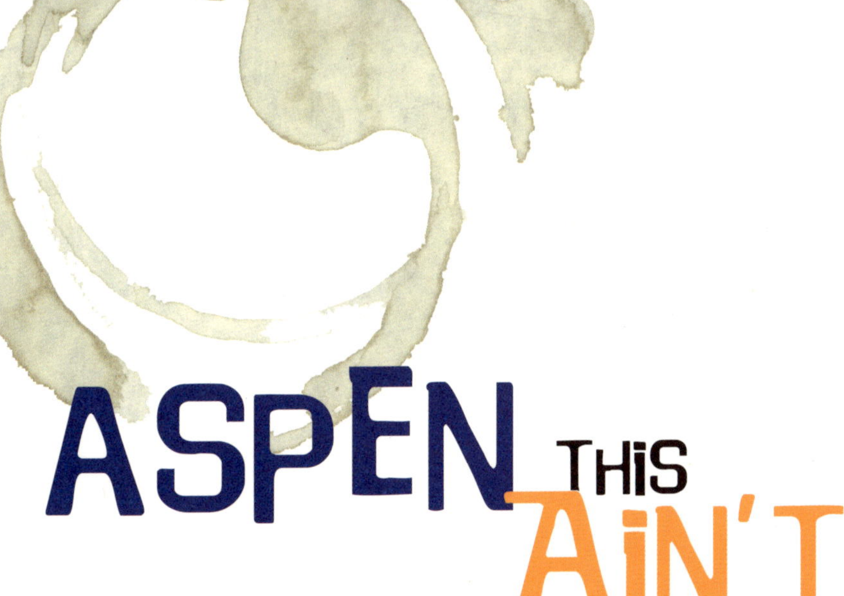

ASPEN THIS AIN'T

The Peace Corps seems to be filled with good-looking, smart, twenty-six-year-old women, and Penny was no exception. She was from Illinois but **spoke Bambara like a native.** It was her job to take Clover's place in Nankorola after Clover left.

The next day the three of us took a **terrifying ride** in a bush taxi from Koutiala to a small road-side stop. There we **caught a donkey cart** and headed west another five kilometers to the village.

Nankorola is an assortment of **a few dozen mud huts,** one dusty road, and a couple hundred **friendly people.** It's surrounded by cotton fields and baobab trees. There is **no electricity** and everyone gets their water from wells. Goats and **donkeys roam free.**

Little kids play everywhere. It's not exactly **picturesque,** but it has a special charm.

An explanation . . .

I once had dinner in Aspen, Colorado, with twelve hungry women—no, not hungry, famished. You wouldn't think women that rich—I'm talking Hershey-chocolate heiress, John Denver's ex-wife, that sort of thing—could get so hungry, but they were starved.

They all lived in an exclusive part of Aspen that they affectionately referred to as Clitwood. They called it Clitwood because almost everyone that lived there was an un-fucking-believably rich, divorced cunt. (I didn't say that, they did. In fact, they said a lot of things that I thought were quite crass, but then what the fuck do I know?) Anyway, I'd won first prize at the Aspen Film Fest, so these nice women had flown me in to be their guest at the festival and have me for dinner.

One of these women took a liking to me. She thought it was charming that I didn't have a pot to piss in. I thought it was annoying that she thought that was charming.

My point is, poverty is not charming, **but the people of Nankorola are.**

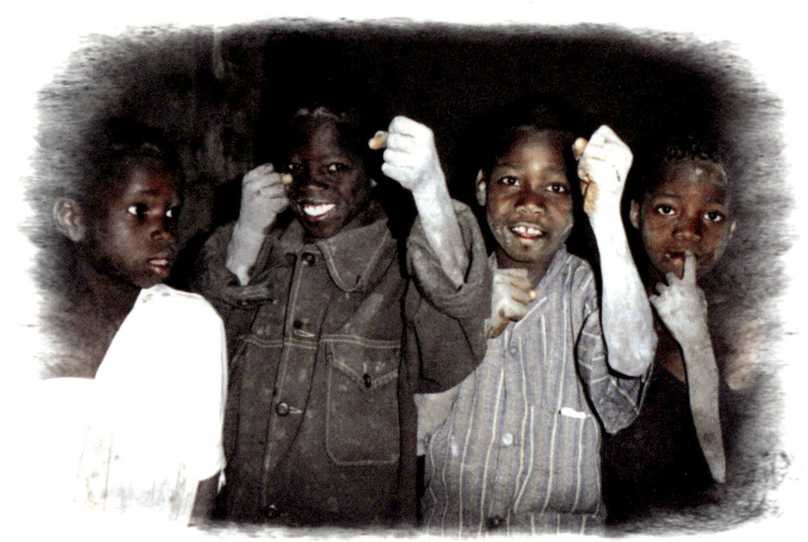

CHILDREN IN NANKOROLA

Penny headed for our house while Clover and I went to greet her African family. We entered a large **mud compound.** The women were grinding millet and cooking. Soulymane, Clover's African father, emerged from behind a small granary. He was a big strong man, **missing a couple of teeth.** It was immediately obvious that Clover adored Soulymane and that he felt the same way about her. Watching them joke and argue was **like watching an old married couple.**

Soulymane **eyed me** for a moment, then shook my hand. Clover introduced me as her father's brother. Later she told me this was necessary because the **people in the village would never understand a single man staying with two single girls.** She mentioned that several people had already inquired about the sleeping arrangements, which, by the way, were me outside on the porch in the **cold** and Clover and Penny snuggled in the house in a big warm bed.

I could go off here about what it's like to be in a bed with two beautiful women, but that would be a lie so I won't . . . except to say that they were twins.

Clover translated as Soulymane asked how old I was. "Forty-five," I replied. He then asked how many children I had. "None," I said. He seemed **puzzled** by this and inquired about my wife. Clover began to stumble through an explanation about how in America some people weren't married. I stopped her midway and asked her to tell Soulymane that my wife had been killed last February in a terrible train **wreck.** Soulymane fell silent for a moment. Then he bestowed numerous blessings upon me. **That was the last time anyone inquired about my marital status.**

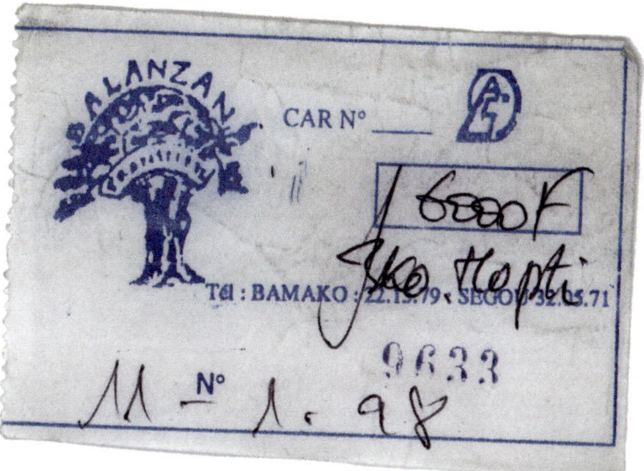

AMERICAN MAGIC

The next day, Clover and I took a walk through the old part of the village, an extremely **spooky place.** Most of the people in Nankorola are Muslim, **but not here.**

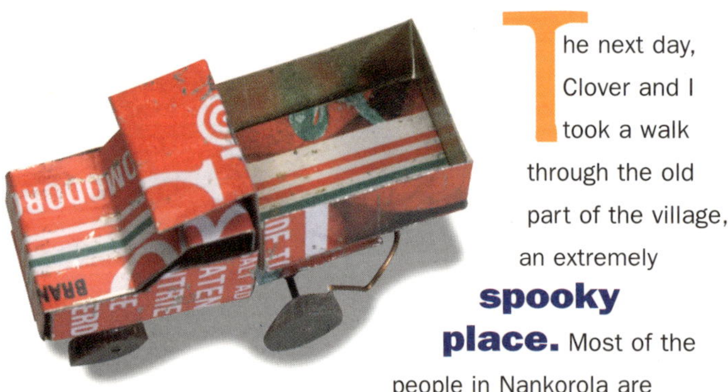

In this part of the village the people are Animists, which means they believe in spirits. I saw a small strange structure with a **pointed roof topped with an ostrich egg.** It looked like a child's playhouse or something that elves would live in. I went to look inside. **"No!"** snapped Clover. I quickly made an about-face and returned to her side. "It is a **forbidden shrine,"** she said. "Don't go in there. Don't take a picture of it. It is not for you."

Later that afternoon I **snuck back to the shrine** by myself. My plan was to **wait until the coast was clear, run into the shrine, snap a photo of what was forbidden, and then run away.** The main obstacles were the **burglar-alarm birds** perched on a wall nearby. Whenever I would get too close to the forbidden shrine, they would start **screeching.**

I threw a stick at the **birds. They ran away.**

I looked around.

No one was in sight.

I ducked inside the shrine and came face to face with a **man in a strange hat** clutching a **fistful of chicken feathers.**

The man looked horrified. I held up my camera. **"Say cheese!"** I said, and the man immediately struck a pose. I clicked his picture and was about to run away when the man spoke to me in English. We left the shrine together and sat beneath a tree nearby.

His name was Adama and he was in a real funk. He told me that **no one in the village liked him** and that no one would invite him to parties. He blamed his problem on a **sorcerer's spell.** I thought for a moment, then pulled my **Redi-teller bankcard** from my wallet and gave it to him. I told him that it was **American magic,** far more powerful than any rinky-dink African spell. I pointed at the hologram on the card's surface and said, "See that eagle, Adama? That is the United States of **America's official bird.**

Anytime

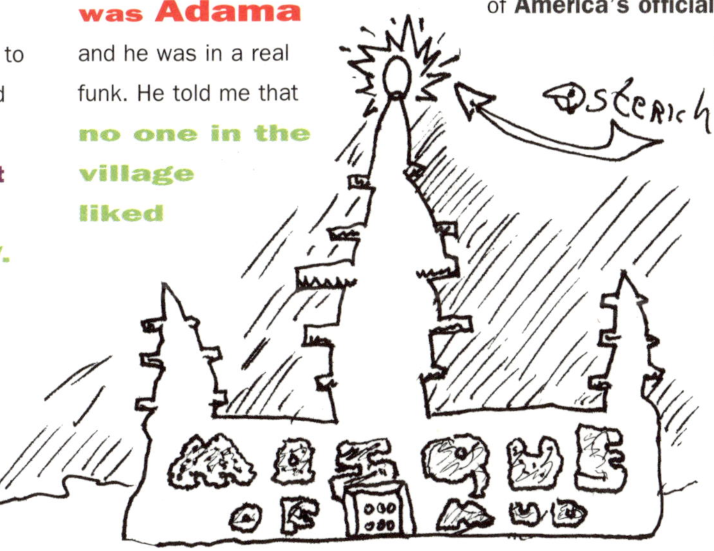

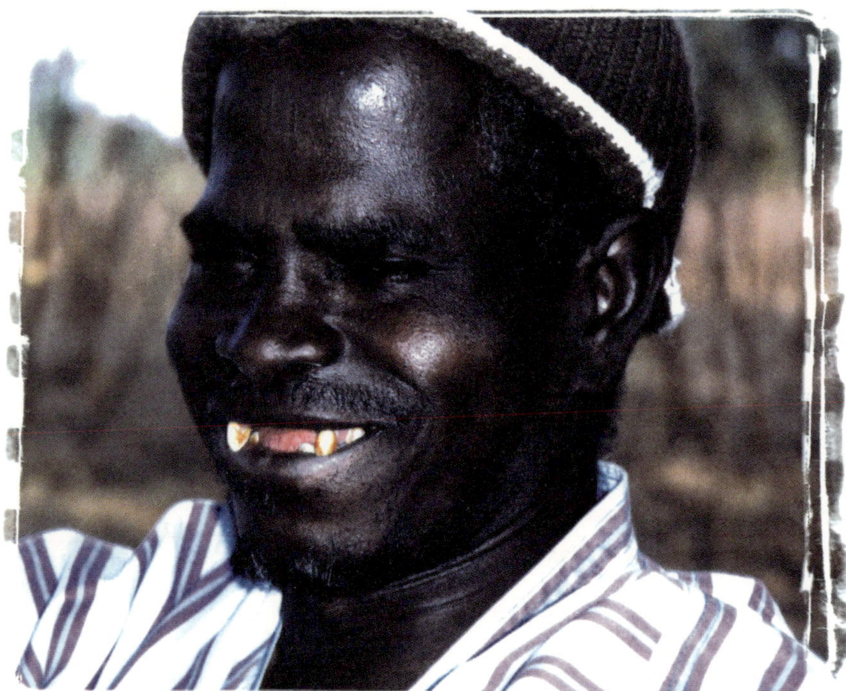

really bugged me, but it wasn't until that moment that I realized what it was. **Lurking** in the back of my mind were **fantasies** of . . . how should I put it . . . something more **romantic happening** between Clover and me.

Well, it wasn't.

Clover treated me like her uncle, and I acted like her uncle, **old Uncle Trent.**

I hated it—and **that** was dangerous.

you feel bad, just **rub that bird** and you'll feel better." Adama seemed impressed. He **rubbed** the eagle with his thumb **and smiled.** "See," I said. "It works."

Adama had heard through the grapevine that I was Clover's uncle. **He hadn't bought the story for one second.** For some reason this made me happy. There was something about the uncle thing that had

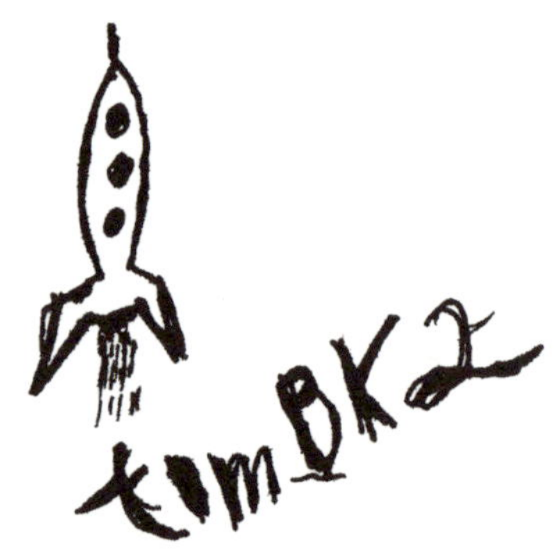

UNCLE PERVERT

LOVE OR FIRE IN YOUR TROUSERS IS NOT EASY TO CONCEAL. SWEDISH PROVERB

It was the end of **Ramadan,** a Muslim holiday and **a big deal** in Nankorola. Everyone puts on their best clothes, visits each other's houses, and feasts.

Clover put on a friend's dress that fit perfectly.

She looked so good it made me nervous. We went to the mosque with the whole village, and **I prayed for a miracle . . .** and lo and behold, a miracle did happen.

Later that afternoon I sat in the kitchen scribbling in my notebook. Clover came in wearing gym

89

shorts and said she was going for a run. **She bent over to tie her shoes,** and suddenly I found myself staring down her T-shirt. She was even more lovely than I had imagined. She began to tie her other shoe, and her T-shirt opened even more. I started to **blush,** then **drool like some dirty old perv** peeking through the bathroom window at his teenage niece. It was **horrible.** But try as I did, I could not turn my eyes from her **breasts.** Finally I stood up. "I need some water," **I squeaked,** and I walked outside.

Later . . .

I sat alone in the bush, thinking. The truth was, the more I got to know Clover, the more I liked her. She

was intelligent. I admired her independence. I appreciated the fact that she liked prostitutes and was trying to save a forgotten language that no one cared about, **and yes, I wanted to tie her to the bed with her panty hose.**

I tried to pump myself up by listing my accomplishments. I was a published author, I'd directed the worst film of the decade, I had two master's degrees, and I'd been **fired from both National Geographic and NBC.** Still, I knew I would not tell Clover the way I felt. It was just too **ridiculous.** And

besides, we would soon be going our separate ways: Clover, back to the guy who studied **chimp turds,** and me, back to my girlfriend in the States. My girlfriend? Oh my God . . . I'd forgotten that I had a girlfriend . . . a wonderful person . . . how could I have forgotten? She's beautiful and never hurts my feelings and I like her very much. And what's more, I don't feel old when I'm around her—and she's two years younger than Clover.

I was so confused at that point that I had to lie down in the dirt.

It was dark when I got back to the house. Clover, Penny, and Soulymane were sitting in lthe kitchen talking. Penny and

Soulymane started **horsing around,** laughing, slugging each other on the shoulder. I watched as Clover turned completely white. **She grabbed her stomach and went outside to throw up.** I waited a minute, then walked out to give her a bottle of water and a flashlight.

I suspected I knew what was going on. Clover was being replaced and she felt it in her guts. Soon she would leave, and Penny would take her house, her job, her place in the village, and, **most painful** of all, Penny would become Soulymane's daughter. It was **heart-breaking** to watch.

Clover pulled it to-gether, made some excuse about **bad food,** and bravely went back inside smiling.

That was impressive.

That was dangerous.

That was the straw that broke the uncle's back.

I was hooked.

That night I went to bed late. I was lying there **counting the ants crawling on my foot** when I heard something out by the road. It was **the goose honk-ing. "Come on, dummy," he said.** "Grab your bagths.

We can thtill make it to the high-way tonight and catch a buths in the morning." I pulled the covers up over my head. **"For hell's thakes,"** the goose yelled, "Leth's go!" "It's too late," **I blubbered.** "Wimp!" the goose hissed. "I sthould have known better than to hook up wif a lightweight like you." And with that the goose picked up his pack. "Stho long, sthucker," he snarled, then **flipped me the bird** and walked off into the night.

Okay, so about this time you're saying to yourself, this guy's turned into a whiny boob. Well, okay, but ah . . . I've been shot at before. In fact, I've been shot at several times. But it wasn't as bad as this. I hated this. And experi-ence told me **it was going to get worse.**

26

THERE'S NO SUCH THING AS A CLEAN GETAWAY

It was like a scene from a movie: the early-morning African sun, red in the dusty sky, the long dirt road, Clover's **eyes swollen with tears,** and me pushing a **bike with a flat tire,** our bags strapped to the back. The plan was to leave before the village woke up, to make it quietly to the highway where we would catch a bus and **head for Mopti.** The plan wasn't working. First Soulymane came out, determined to walk with us to the highway. Then his brother ran out crying, then his wife came out crying, and then, one by one, **dozens of**

emerged from the mud huts. Everyone was **wailing** and hugging. Even Soulymane's **dog whimpered.**

I walked on ahead by myself.

Finally Soulymane, Clover, and I made it to the highway. We sat down at a roadside stand and ordered hot mike and bread.

Clover drank and ate, then said, "Trent, I've decided to go back to Koutiala by myself. You can catch a bus here for Mopti."

"Oh . . . of course," I said. "That makes sense."

"I need a rest," she went on. "I'm completely **drained."**

"Sure," I said, "I understand."

We waited together for a while. A bush taxi finally came, and Clover climbed on board. "Soulymane will stay here with you," she said. "He will put you on the right bus." "Right," I said. **"No problem."** "Maybe I'll see you in Bamako," she said. I smiled, but I knew the chances

were slim. The **bush taxi rattled away** and left Soulymane and me standing in the **stupid** dust.

We sat for a while, and I drank a **stupid** Coke.

Soulymane tried on my **stupid** sunglasses.

Then he walked over by a tree, stood for a moment, and then walked back. He pointed to another bush taxi coming down the road and motioned for me to get up. "No," I said. "I'm getting on the bus, the bus to Mopti." Soulymane kept pointing at the bush taxi and saying, **"Mopti! Mopti!"** I knew there were no bush taxis to Mopti so I latched hold of my chair and said, **"No. No. Bus! I want bus!"** **Soulymane grabbed my bag** and **threw it** on top of the taxi. Then he yanked me out of my

seat and pushed me into the old truck. "Mopti," he said, and he waved good-bye.

The bush taxi pulled out, turned, and headed in the wrong direction. Almost immediately we passed the right bus going in the right direction on its way to Mopti. "That **dirty bastard!"** I screamed. "He couldn't wait one more minute?!"

An hour later **I found myself in Koutiala,** hurrying down the road looking for a

WILD-GOOSE

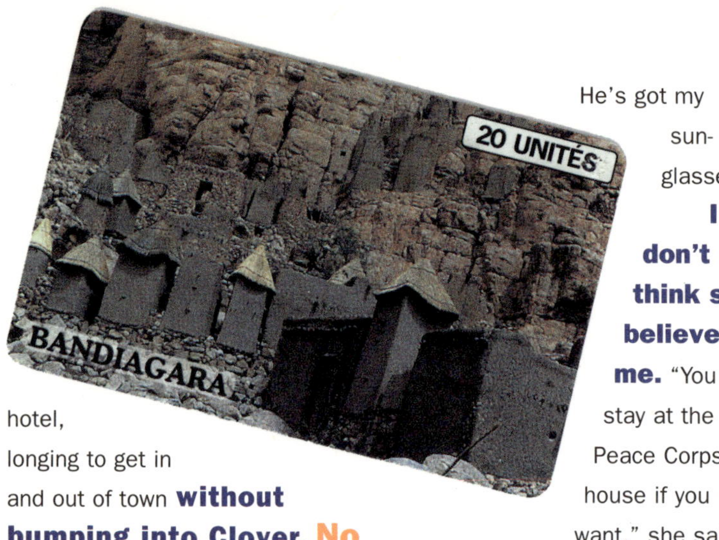

hotel, longing to get in and out of town **without bumping into Clover. No such luck.** Here she came, walking down the street towards me. "What are you doing here?" she asked. I started to rant. "It's all his fault! It's not my fault! I grabbed my chair! I said Mopti! Mopti! **But noooo! He took my bag!** I said give me back my bag! And then I saw the bus going the other way! I tried to **jump off!** I'm really not a bad penny! **Soulymane's an ass!**

He's got my sunglasses!" **I don't think she believed me.** "You can stay at the Peace Corps house if you want," she said. "No, absolutely not," I countered. "I'm checking into a hotel!" Then she said, "I'm glad I ran into you. I want you to mail something for me when you get back to the States." She reached into her bag and handed me a postcard. Of course, I immediately read it. It said, *Happy Valentine's Day, Love, Clover,* and it was addressed to her boyfriend. "Sure! I'd be **happy as hell** to mail this," I said, and with that I picked up my bag, bade a fond farewell, found a room, locked the door, turned on the radio, and started to dance . . . **then I threw up.**

My God, I said to myself, **I've become a blubbering pathetic dork.**

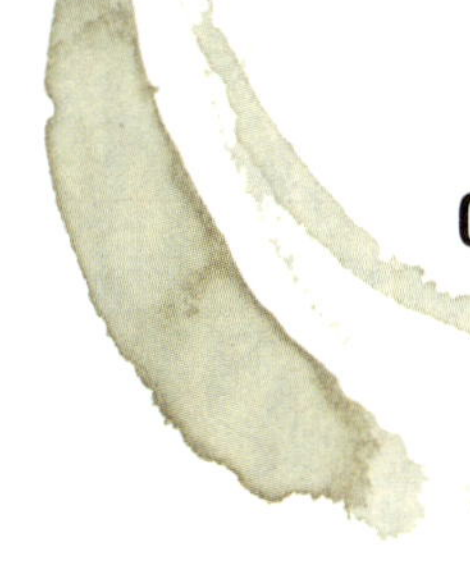

BACK IN BAMAKO AGAIN

It took a few days, but **I finally made it back to Bamako** and checked in to a hotel. I had forty-eight **hours to kill** before my plane to the States, so I went for a walk and ran into my old friends **Bill Cosby** and **John Travolta.** We were sitting by the river talking when somehow **the conversation turned to women.** Of course, both Cosby and Travolta were **married** to **their cousins,** so they had absolutely no idea what it was like to feel like an uncle. They did, however, convince me that what I knew about the opposite **sex** could easily **fit up an ant's ass.** They also

95

knew where the Bamako Peace Corps house was and, despite my protests, **dragged** me there.

I didn't really think Clover was in town, but on the off chance that she was, I left a note with detailed instructions on how to find me.

Late that night Clover **showed up at my hotel.** We went to dinner and drank a bottle of wine. Clover got a little **tipsy** and began to ask me what I considered personal questions. Did I have a girlfriend? What was she like? Why hadn't I taken her with me on my trip? I **ducked and dodged** and managed to get away **without really answering** anything. Then she asked me why I had never been married. I said, "Oh, I don't know. It never seemed like a very good idea." Then I said, "I have, however, had many wonderful girlfriends." She looked at me for a moment and then said, "If a man has had thirty-two girlfriends in twenty years, is he successful with women or a failure?" **I felt my sphincter slam shut.** Good Lord, I thought, this girl really likes to **go for the throat.** But then my mind began to race . . . Nancy, Beth, Barbara, Stephene, Michelle, Laura, Julie, Judy, Joleen, Allison, Annie, Lisa, TC, Valerie, Pam, Linda, and all the others . . . what had happened? Many had simply gotten bored and moved on. One had run away and **joined the circus.** Two had full-blown **nervous breakdowns.** Then there was Debbie, the ballet dancer from Texas with a **syrupy-sweet** accent and big brown eyes. I'd perhaps loved her most

Abdoul Salam TRAORE

Marchand Arts Africain
au Marché de N'golonina Mag. N° 87 . 88

BP : 1038
Tel :

Bamako
Rép. du Mali

of all, and I'd left her standing in an airport while I **went off to Hollywood with the wild goose.**

I laughed nervously and ordered more wine.

We walked through the dark back to Clover's place. I nearly gave her a hug, but I figured she would **kick me in the nuts** so I **decided against it.**

THE LAST DAY

LOVE IS A DARK PIT. HUNGARIAN PROVERB

It was **hot and dusty.** I was feeling very **strange,** and Clover was looking a bit **ragged** herself. We walked around for a while, not really knowing what to do. We stopped at a fruit stand, and the **vendor asked Clover if I was her father.** Clover laughed and said yes. I laughed too. **I laughed real hard.**

I had told Clover that I was writing a book about my trip. Now she asked how it was going. "Not so good," I said. "I've been so **overwhelmed** by everything that has happened to me in Africa that I am having a **hard time focusing** my thoughts." Clover suggested she take her cassette recorder and interview me, then give me the tape so I could listen to it later. She believed that might help me **center my ideas.** At first I thought this was a good idea, but as we made our way back to my hotel I broke out in a **cold sweat. Some rocks you just don't want to look under.**

We found a small boat near my hotel, and the captain motored us to the center of the Niger. Clover turned on her recorder and **began the interview.** First she asked me why I had ventured to Africa. I told her I was seeking **excitement and danger.** She asked me if I had found any. I said, only her. "What do you mean by that?" she said. I changed the subject. Then she said, "I know you **admire dogs** because they are loyal, but that seems weird because loyalty obviously isn't important to you." **I was so befuddled I nearly fell in the river.** She went on, "What kind of woman are you looking for?" I couldn't answer that either. She

FOOLS AND MADMEN SPEAK THE TRUTH.

ENGLISH PROVERB

asked me if I ever saw myself becoming a father. **I giggled and muttered something stupid.** "Why can't you sit in one place very long? Do you consider yourself stable? What is really important to you?" I stammered while **she continued to pound me with questions.** "Where are you going next? Do you think you'll find what you're looking for there? How will you know it when you find it?" I tried to explain but couldn't.

Then I asked her a question. "Why did you invite me to come with you to your village?" "Because," she said, "I wanted someone from the outside world to see what I was seeing." "Yes," I said, "but why me?" She studied me for a moment and then said, "I asked a lot of people to go. You were the only one to take me up on the offer." There was a **long silence.** Then Clover said, "It seems like you're holding something back, Trent. What is it you really want to say?" I **stared at the water** for a long time and then said, "No, I'm not holding anything back."

THE FINAL CHAPTER

HE WHO DEPARTS IS FORGOTTEN DAILY. JAPANESE PROVERB

HE WHO GOES AND RETURNS
MAKES A GOOD JOURNEY.

FRENCH PROVERB

There are times in a man's life when he just has to say, **"How the fuck did I ever get here doing this?"** Well, waiting for the bus with Clover in front of my hotel was **one of those times for me.**

I decided to take one more crack at explaining myself.

"You know, Clover," I started, "I'm really not that big of a mess . . .

"I mean, I'm **not** responsible . . .

"I mean . . . sure . . . sometimes I go over here, and then I go over there, but, ah . . .

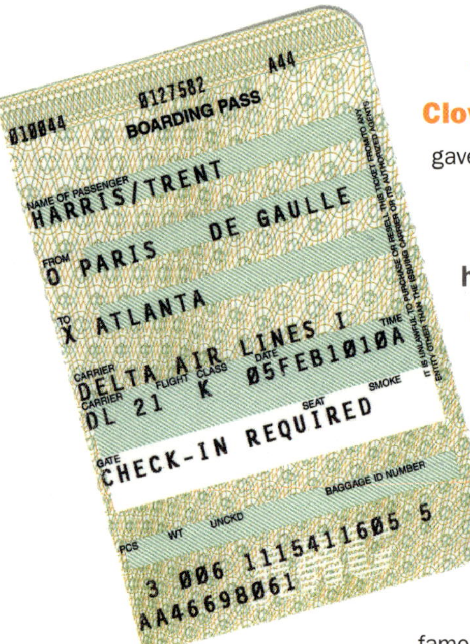

"What you have to understand, Clover, is . . . I have a bad case of the Huckleberry Finn syndrome."

"No shit, Sherlock," she said, and I shut up.

Finally the bus came. **I stalled and muttered.**

The driver revved his engine impatiently.

I kicked the dirt, **fiddled** with my jacket, looked at my feet.

Then I grabbed Clover. I pulled her close. I gave her a big hug.

Then I gave her another. I was **about to drag her** onto the bus with me and take her to the airport where we would **catch a plane to Paris,** settle down in a château, and have dozens of beautiful children with names like Fatima and Soulymane. There I would become a famous film director loved by the French, and she would save Miniakan for all the world. But then **she looked at me and with a sly smile said, "So long, uncle."**

"Oh, for hell's sakes," I said, and **I got on the bus and left.**

The plane leaped off the runway and into the night. I looked out my window and watched **Africa fade into the hollow blackness.** I sat back in my seat and took note.

My clothes were filthy. My shoes had holes. My stomach was in my throat, and I suspected I was coming down with malaria.

In short, **I felt and smelt like an elephant** had just **crapped on my chest.**

Yes, I had to admit it. It had been a successful trip.

I had **fought my way** through the land of the runaway pygmies, **survived the attack** of the giant parrots,

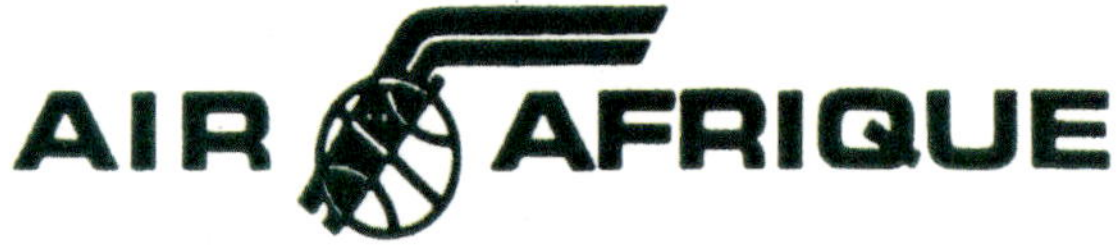

repelled the advances of **sex-starved lesbians,** and even **sniffed** the **scabbards** of the Tuareg rebels. I had grabbed the bull by the tail, **kicked the bear in the butt,** screamed in the porcupine's ear, and when it came to Clover, scared the **bejesus** right out

of myself.

I had accomplished my goal. **I would be a better man.**

I knew it.

Jane put it best when she said, **"If it doesn't kill Tarzan, it makes Tarzan happy."**

I was happy all right. I was so happy I could hardly stand it. I looked around the cabin of the plane and said to myself, "So this is what it's like to be sane." It felt good, so I ordered a **gin and tonic** from the giraffe running down the aisle.

Suddenly **the plane dropped** down out of the night and made an **unscheduled stop** in Nouakchott, the capital of Mauritania. **The wild goose got on board and sat**

down next to me. He took off his sunglasses, adjusted his turban, and said, "Stho, did you make a fool of yourthelf?" "Yes," I said **proudly.** "Good," he hissed. Then he threw a magazine in my lap. I opened it up to a photograph of a jungle. **"The Amathzon,"** he whispered. "We'll find headhuntethrs and pink dolphthins." I looked the goose square in the eye and said, "You, sir, are an **ass wipe!"** The goose pointed at the photo again. "The dolphthins thwim in the Orinoco River and hardly anybody ever sees 'em." "I can't go to the Amazon!" I said. "I'm broke, I'm tired, and I think I'm having a **midlife crisis."** **"Horth thit,"** said the goose. "Bethides, ith's not that expenthive. One way is lesth than five hundred buckths." "One way!" I yelled. "Round trip then," snarled the goose.

"It sthill won't clip you more than a grand." I **sank down** in my seat and hid my face in my hands. I thought to myself, **perhaps I'll just strangle the ugly bas-tard** right now.

After all, it's not against the law to **kill a goose,** especially one that's such an **annoying dink.**

I looked up.

The goose was **guzzling** my peanuts.

"You swear they're pink?" I said.

The goose smiled.

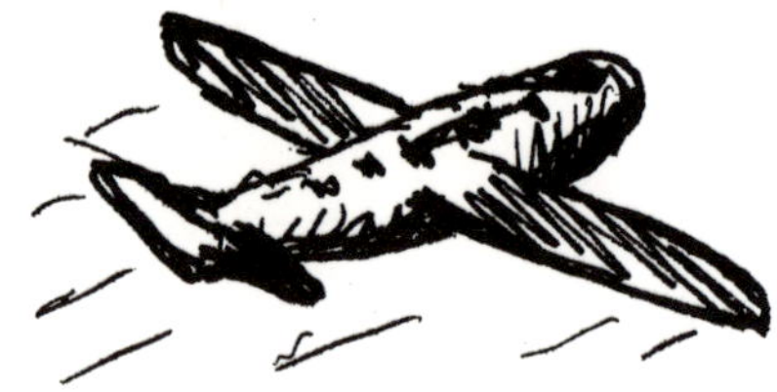